# COACHING LEADS FORMULA

HOW TO GO FROM COACHING
**PART TIME TO *FULL TIME***
USING A PROVEN 6-STEP FORMULA

THEO BILL

Coaching Leads Formula
Copyright © 2022 by Theo Bill

All rights reserved. No part of this book may be used or reproduced in any form whatsoever without written permission except in the case of brief quotations in critical articles or reviews.

Printed in the United States of America.

Book and Cover design by Theo Bill

**To download the audiobook version & find out more, go to: https://getcfl.com/audio**

# Table of Contents

1. Introduction ............................................................ 1
2. The Business ........................................................... 7
3. Branding Fundamentals ........................................... 15
4. Your Marketing Plan ............................................... 19
    Engagement Cycle ................................................. 20
    Coaching Leads Formula ....................................... 22
    Marketing Assets ................................................... 22

5. The CLF Recipe ..................................................... 27
6. Dream Client Identity............................................. 33
    Target Niche.......................................................... 35
    Client Identity ....................................................... 36

7. Conversation Hook................................................. 46
8. Your Hero's Journey............................................... 55
9. Website ................................................................. 63
10. Landing Page ....................................................... 67
    Hero Section.......................................................... 69
    Consequences ....................................................... 72
    Benefits................................................................. 74
    Authority .............................................................. 76
    The Map................................................................ 78
    Reinforcement ...................................................... 81
    Video ................................................................... 82
    Putting It All Together .......................................... 84

11. Lead Magnet........................................................ 87

12. Get The Word Out................................................ 95
    Next Steps ............................................................ 95
    Where and How.................................................... 96

13. Thank You Page................................................... 99
14. Magic of Email.................................................... 103
    Broadcast Emails ................................................ 104
    Why Sequence It?................................................ 105

Sales Sequences .............................................. 108
Nurture Sequence ......................................... 111

15. Your Offer.................................................. 119
Pricing ......................................................... 125

16. Sales Psychology.......................................... 131
Building Rapport......................................... 133
Identifying Needs ........................................ 133
Link the Need to Coaching........................... 135
Objections.................................................... 135

17. Back Office.................................................. 139
Onboarding Process ..................................... 139
Tracking Client Progress.............................. 143
Retaining Clients.......................................... 144
Virtual Offices ............................................. 147

18. Testimonials ................................................ 149
19. Wrapping it Up ............................................ 153
20. Resources.................................................... 157

# Forward

For some time now, I've had people tell me they enjoyed my writing or when I give a presentation how much they like it. I'm always flattered and a little surprised by their opinion though.

When I was young, a great uncle said I had a "mellifluous" way of speaking. He explained to me (because I had no idea the meaning) that it meant a "pleasant way of speaking or communicating." I don't know if he meant my words or my voice, but I took it as a great compliment. Until now though, I've never had the courage to put anything out there with the scope of this book - like many of my (and I imagine your) clients, I doubted myself.

As I began to write this, something miraculous happened! The words just started to flow! It was easy and enjoyable. I found that when I asked people about it, they enjoyed reading it and that I had an easy way of explaining things so they could understand it.

Marketing, design, sales, and copywriting are all skills I've acquired over time - many of the ideas in this book aren't new. I've had the joy and honor to learn from some masters - Andre Chaperon for email, the great Gary Halpern for copywriting, Russell Brunson for perfecting the art of the funnel, as well as Robert Cialdini, Don Miller, Neil Patel, Seth Godin, and Ryan Deiss are just some from whom I've learned a great deal.

In a nutshell, marketing is about communication - how do we have a conversation with our prospects? Instead of something difficult or something you dread, I hope to show you it can be something fun and rewarding! We often complicate it though. I hope this book serves to simplify and demystify that process for you.

I've had a lot of help putting this book together with some very talented and important people, but I couldn't neglect to thank the most important one in my life - my mother. Her eye for detail and willingness (some might say duty) to question me, was invaluable. And her never-ending support and encouragement is something I'm grateful for each and every day.

INTRODUCTION

# 1. Introduction

Once upon a time I was in a very dark place in my life. I imagine some of you reading this may have visited this place. The demons and desert of the unknown lay spread out before me. I had no guide or confidence that I could cross that unknowable expanse to find peace and happiness again.

Then I met a coach. That coach changed my life and helped me see that he had crossed that desert himself, and that there were others who had come before him who showed him the way and were waiting for me on the other side of the expanse.

He showed me that all it took was finding the tools and skills I needed. That coach helped me focus on new goals, new meanings, and new beliefs.

My coach showed me by example that there are people out there who—every day—step up, demand more of themselves and, in the process, help others' lives transform. I was humbled and honored by that coach and my life was set upon a new path. This book is simply another step in that new direction.

## COACHING LEADS FORMULA

I embarked upon that path because I wanted to help people. I imagine you understand that need - that drive. I'm betting you've always had a desire to help and assist others. When I first discovered coaching and how powerful it is, and as I encountered how accessible the training and tools are, I was hooked.

Imagine for a moment, a world where 250 million people know and utilize the tools of awareness, conscious action, compassion and, as a result, live healthier lifestyles! What an incredible world that would be!

According to the 3.5% rule (meaning how many people are needed to change society's prevailing opinions), that's all it takes to change the world!

Imagine if we could open up the awareness of the entire world to become a better place? If YOU personally (through a group coaching program, 1:1 clients, or in your greater business) reach JUST one hundred clients per year for ten years, this message only needs to reach and inspire 250,000 coaches! That's why I'm writing this book and why I'm passionate about coaching—because I understand the struggle and the pain many of you and many of your clients have experienced or have moved past.

Back in 2015 I was 40 lbs overweight, depressed, and borderline suicidal. I was going through a divorce, facing possible bankruptcy, AND moving not only my personal home but a business and farm as well! Many people only experience two or three of those stress factors over a lifetime. I experienced them all at once!

I was paralyzed. I didn't want to admit that I needed help. But as a result of an ultimatum, I faced my deepest fear and sought out help. I had such deep-seated resistance because I thought that if I couldn't figure it out myself, it meant *I was broken.*

Useless…*Worthless.*

# INTRODUCTION

Eventually I sought out help and stopped being a victim of my own fear.

It was a coach who gave me tools to handle the challenges I was facing.

My physical and mental health slowly began to improve as I used the tools I was learning every day.

I believe healing can come from the inside out or from the outside in. If you're a health coach or a life coach, you have the power to create massive healing in the world by helping your clients.

I know you're a coach because you want to help people.

Take a look at these staggering statistics, which I feel the coaching industry is equipped to combat. Did you know (as of 2021) in America alone:

- 42% are pre-diabetic (that's 138 million)

- 74% of adults over 20 are either overweight or obese (that's 244 million! )

- 10% experience depression (30 million!)

- 20% are diagnosed with anxiety (60 million!)

Even if there's a bit of overlap between those statistics, that's still well over 250 million people in America whose lives can literally be saved by coaches just like you.

Let me ask you, why are you reading this book? I'm guessing it's because you want to generate more leads, right? And you'd also like a comfortable (or maybe wealthy) lifestyle?

I'm guessing it's also because YOU want to help people, right?

My goal is to get you (at a bare minimum) between four and eight consistent clients paying you each and every month.

## COACHING LEADS FORMULA

Why that number? Because that's all it should take to get you across the $60k mark, which, in much of the country, is the minimum income needed to support yourself doing what you love.

Think about that—that's ALL you need in order to be able to quit your regular job and pursue coaching with your full attention. You can make much more than $60k, but that's just the start.

Look at how easy that "full-time" income can be:

- 2 client packages @$2,500 per month = $60,000
- 5 weekly coaching clients @$250/hr = $62,500 *(with a vacay)*
- 8 clients @$50/session 3x a week = $60,000

I think you'll agree that if you put your mind to it, and with the tools you will learn in this book, getting to $60k a year is pretty achievable, no matter the type of coaching you do!

Here's the bonus: With those numbers above, you even get a paid two-week vacation!

How's that for living the dream…all from working a max of sixteen hours a week.

I know everyone's definition of happy is different. But with that schedule, what would you be able to do with the rest of your time? Some of the coaches I've worked with like to:

- Spend quality time with loved ones
- Continue to grow and learn
- Volunteer for passion causes
- Attend networking events
- Give a Tedx talk
- Research new projects (like a book)

# INTRODUCTION

Because you get to take control of your life by having time to focus on the important things (like building and growing your business, not just chasing your tail), it gives you more time for clients, family, friends, or whatever else makes you happy and fulfilled.

Obviously pricing and packages are a much larger conversation, but if you thought it wasn't possible to coach full time or that it was for other people but not you, I hope you now see how easily it can be for you too.

Of course the hours you're coaching isn't all the time you will spend on your business; there will be administrative activities you'll need to do. But at least you won't have to spend time getting clients in the door! There's an old saying: "There's few problems that good cash flow can't solve!" With enough clients, you'll be able to hire an assistant for things you don't want to do.

I want you to be able to do what makes you happy. That means changing lives, making an impact, relieving pain and suffering through healthier habits or choices—mental and physical. For many of you, money is simply the beginning.

To get to your happy place, you must be able to support yourself. The saying, "place the oxygen mask on yourself before your child," applies here too. You've got to be able to support your basic needs before you can start to truly change the world.

If you aren't already, you need to be proficient with your skills and tools, but once you have that, a business won't magically appear before your eyes. It can be done: - As Tony Robbins says, "Success leaves clues." When you follow the rainbow, you will find your pot of gold.

So what's the catch, you ask? This book is designed to give you the tools. Tools are wonderful things, but even the most expensive drill is utterly useless if it collects dust.

## COACHING LEADS FORMULA

Start off slow and methodically by following the book and you will create that life you dream of and deserve. When you have mastered step one, move on to step two, and so forth. Don't get stuck in being overwhelmed or thinking it doesn't apply. Just do the work and you'll unearth that pot of gold in no time!

If you want to be a successful coach, you need three things:

1. Experience & proficiency

2. Motivation to serve

3. The right dream client & niche

Because the coaching industry is an unregulated one (and in my mind that's a good thing), there are coaches *without* the experience and proficiency.

I already know that's not you. That type of coach wouldn't have picked up this book.

YOU are a passionate, qualified, and powerful coach who wants to grow with and for your clients. You already have a motivation and desire to serve your clients. You are courageous in the face of your own fears and your clients' fears as well!

With all that said, I'm honored to meet you, dear reader, dear coach, dear life-changing-force-for-amazing-good!

In the next chapter we'll talk about the importance of having a business mindset.

As Dr. Who might say, "Allons-y"!

# 2. The Business

I attended a business education seminar where the speaker asked everyone in the room (there were about 5,000 participants in the room) to stand up if they've been in business for more than a year. Then he asked folks to remain standing if they've been in business for 5 years, then 10 years. To my surprise, while I remained standing, I watched as nearly 95% of the room sat back down. But then he asked how many of those businesses had at least $100,000 in annual sales (not profit, mind you). He repeated it with $500,000 and then $1,000,000 a year. To my shock, I was still standing with the select few who had remained on their feet.

When you do the math on the statistics, I was in a tiny minority of business owners - those who had been in business for over 10 years and earned over $1 million per year. I was in the 0.001 part of the statistics - one tenth of one percent! I had beaten the odds of so many other entrepreneurs!

I'm not sharing this to show off but rather to illustrate that I know how difficult building a business can be! I've been there, and have the bruises to prove it! Business is a rough sport, but it's also one that is rewarding beyond compare for those who love it. But not all coaches consider themselves to be in business.

## COACHING LEADS FORMULA

Coaching and being in the *business* of coaching are vastly different animals. To simply *be a coach*, all you need is to be willing to coach someone. To have a *coaching business*, you must have a sound business plan and/or model in place. Otherwise you will find yourself in the same group of over 75% of the rest of the coaching industry making less than $25k a year. I don't know about you, but I couldn't support myself on only $25,000. I'd have to have a second job just to pay my mortgage!

As we talked about earlier though, getting to the magic $60k mark is quite realistic when you break it down. And once you have a consistent flow of leads who turn into clients, it'll be even easier! There's no right or wrong way to get there, but there are specific ways that have led to success with the coaches I've worked with, which I'll share with you in this book.

I'll restate my goal here—to get you to at least $60k (full-time income). If you're doing anything less, you're simply getting paid for a hobby, not a profession. And I want to work with committed coaches who really have a desire to change the world!

So, how do you do it?

Here's the secret (drum roll please!):

The best way to have a coaching BUSINESS is to have a consistent pipeline of clients!

That's it. I know, quite the let down, no? It's not sexy or going to happen overnight, but it's reliable and consistent. AND it guarantees you will have a business and life you love with time for the people in your life and for the activities you want to do.

To me, that's called freedom.

Yes, high-ticket sales are great and you see tons of ads for them—and you can get a client overnight. I offer high-ticket coaching; it's rewarding, but it's also very intense (in terms of time and energy).

## THE BUSINESS

If all you do is high-ticket packages, you have an uphill battle acquiring customers because that's typically a long sales cycle. And worse, if one client goes on vacation or decides not to renew with you (or God forbid wants a refund), a huge chunk of your income just went to Florida and is drinking a beer on the beach!

Think of the high-ticket clients as cream on the top of your reliable, consistent other clients. Once you get consistent and more experienced (in the coaching and the sales part of the equation), you can, of course, raise your rates (if you choose) or even focus more on the high-ticket folks.

But for now, let's focus on the lower-price-point clients. With the lower price point comes an easier sales conversation and more clients as well. That translates into consistent, reliable, predictable income—the hallmark of a good business!

Many coaches I talk with want to 1) help clients and 2) quit their day job so they can coach full-time. The average advertisement of "becoming a coach" brings up images of a coach sitting on the beach drinking a margarita with the palms swaying in the background or sitting on a private jet clinking champagne glasses.

But the reality is far different. As few as 10-25% of coaches are able to pay their bills by doing what they love. And sadly, many abandon it after less than a year of trying (and failing) to get clients.

It is my hope and goal that YOU land in that top tier of coaches living life on your terms, living a life of freedom—whatever that means to you. But before you get there, you will need to master your mindset around business and money.

I'm certain you know how to help your clients with their challenges, struggles, and goals, but when you're facing your own challenges, how often do you "coach" yourself? I can't tell you how many coaches I've spoken with who, if they simply listened to themselves, would be far more successful and happy.

COACHING LEADS FORMULA

On my wall over my whiteboard for the past five years, I have written, "What would I say to a client about that?" whenever I'm facing a challenge. I invite you to apply your coaching skills to your own unique challenges and thought patterns. Put yourself in your own client's shoes and ask yourself, "Is that REALLY true?" or "How could this be easy?"

In business, and yes you're in business, the biggest challenge is often fear, which can manifest in many ways. I've noticed fear often manifests itself in three big ways: through overcomplicating things, perfectionism, and imposter syndrome.

I call these three the Big Business Bullies. How do you win a fight with a bully? By confronting it! Take a moment and ask yourself, "What am I afraid of?" when something seems to have too many steps, or you feel you're not good enough, or you think you need more education or certifications before you can do something.

Our schoolyard hero against the Big Business Bullies can also be the Superhero Simplicity! The simpler you keep things, the less you have to worry about complications. You can forget about the need for it to be perfect. You don't need to worry about a long, detailed explanation that only a PhD could decipher because you kept things SIMPLE!

## "SIMPLICITY IS THE ULTIMATE SOPHISTICATION."
### LEONARDO DA VINCI

The more complicated things get, the more apt something is to go wrong (the old KISS rule).

# THE BUSINESS

The biggest worry many have about simplicity is that they made the wrong decision. Well guess what? That's life! However, if you learn something from it, then it's actually to your benefit. But if you calculated, composed, and complicated it for weeks on end, you will learn nothing, because chances are you won't take action - you'll be stuck in analysis paralysis. That would be a terrible shame, because I want you to change lives!

Problems arise when we start to complicate things. One example of making it too complicated: You might think, "I have to make six figures" to be happy.

Horsepoo.

Six figures is a made-up number some marketing genius thought of. It has no bearing on your actual cost of living, your dreams, or your goals. Figure out YOUR real number that can cover your expenses and add a bit on top for emergencies. THAT is your freedom number.

It might not be $60k. It might only be $30k! I don't know. That's entirely up to you to decide. But once you hit it—and I have a feeling you'll exceed it—you will have systems in place that will allow you to decide exactly how much you want to work and not work.

Again, that sounds like freedom to me!

With what you're going to learn in this book, and if you follow what I tell you, you WILL have that freedom.

Another complication can be software (I can hear the groans now, but have no fear). There are many options out there for various software solutions. In the end, software is simply a tool—and if one doesn't work for you or doesn't work the way you need, you can choose another. I'll mention some software I recommend and use in the resources section of this book.

## COACHING LEADS FORMULA

For now, don't get bogged down in thinking you need to go out and analyze every software and subscription out there. Some are amazingly useful and have a list of features a mile long. I want you focused on your top three or four needs though. If you know the top three or four things you need the software to do and it does them, then good enough!

As I heard Uri Levine, the founder of Waze, say: "Good enough is good enough." Any better than that and you've probably lost momentum; any worse than that and you probably won't have a fit with your customer.

Remember, you're in business. Businesses have expenses. Businesses also have employees and, although you're the primary one, you can hire others to help you along the way. There are virtual assistants, graphic designers, video editors, administrative assistants, social media managers—all sorts of people who can help you! Don't let not knowing how to do something (or not being comfortable with it) stop your progress—find a way to get it done. There ARE resources out there that can allow you to achieve your goals.

You're not alone, unless you want to be.

The most insidious way that we get stopped before even beginning is what I consider probably the most debilitating bully: Imposter Syndrome.

If you're a film fan, you may have seen the movie (or read the book even) *Catch Me If You Can*, which was about a con man, Frank Abagnale, Jr. (played by Leo DiCaprio in the film). There's a scene where he's teaching a university-level class on sociology. When he was caught by the authorities, Frank (the real one) was asked, "How did you convince the students and other professors you were qualified to teach?"

## THE BUSINESS

His response is priceless and it shows how powerful a little knowledge can be. He told the officer, "I read one chapter ahead of the students." He wasn't a master of sociology, but he knew just a little more than the students did, and he still had a big impact on their lives.

I feel it's important to offer an alternative reframe for Imposter Syndrome because it's so powerful and limits so many people.

Several years ago I had the opportunity to visit Sedona, Arizona. For those of you who haven't gone before, it's breathtaking. The landscapes, energy, and rugged beauty of the area make it a destination for healers, energy workers, and outdoor enthusiasts.

There is a magical rock formation called Cathedral Rock, which has one of the energy vortexes that make Sedona famous. The hike to get to the vortex can be quite rigorous and difficult, but I was determined to get there and experience this energy vortex for myself!

I had been hiking for about an hour and got to a point where people had gotten backed up and were waiting for people ahead to move up the slope. Eventually I got past the sticking point and learned why there was the hold-up—it was a pretty steep and difficult spot on the trail.

Once I had gotten past the rough spot though, I heard a woman calling out to her husband behind me. She was having difficulty getting up the path and it was clear her husband wasn't able to help her.

I had two choices: leave her to her (unhelpful) husband, or help her up.

If I had decided I first had to get to the very top of the mountain in order to feel adequate to assist her, she probably would have turned around and gone back to the car, disappointed and hurt that she couldn't accomplish what she wanted.

## COACHING LEADS FORMULA

But of course, I didn't need to get all the way to the top in order to help her. I had just been up that section of the path and knew exactly what she needed to do in order to get farther along her path, so I helped her and she was incredibly grateful for the assistance.

The next time you're confronted by a feeling of comparison or Imposter Syndrome, remember those metaphors. I hope they will be enough to keep you going when you feel like you might quit.

# 3. Branding Fundamentals

Sometimes coaches think that branding, sales, and marketing are all the same. They're not.

There is a process that a total stranger will undertake to become your client. Along the way, you will have a conversation with them to build more and more rapport until they swipe their credit card. The first part of that conversation is called marketing and the later phase of the conversation is called sales.

Along the path of that conversation, there will be various cues the prospect will encounter (signs, advertisements, websites, etc.) that will all have a certain look and feel. That is branding.

Marketing, sales, and branding are relatives of the same family tree (your business), but they're not the same at all. Many coaches think that branding is more important than marketing.

I would disagree.

I feel branding IS important, but less so than having a good, solid marketing plan.

## COACHING LEADS FORMULA

Imagine two scenarios:

1. I came up to you, well-dressed and looking like a million bucks, but started speaking very fast in a foreign language you couldn't understand.

2. I came up to you looking like I just got my clothes from the Salvation Army, but we had a fascinating conversation and it was like I could practically read your thoughts.

Which person would you think would be most interesting to you? You might have initially thought the well-dressed person interesting, but they didn't hold your attention because they didn't speak your language. But the other person who didn't look so hot but knew all the right things to say...I'm guessing that is the one who would win your time and affection.

Of course, the hope is to look great AND say all the right things. But this book is more about marketing than branding. With that in mind, I want to say a few words about branding.

Branding has to do with fonts, colors, images, logos, headlines, and other design elements. It also has to do with your product or service name. Although you can easily change it at any time, if you choose a good one early on, it will benefit you down the line. You won't have the expense and headache of having to rebrand, but even better, it will draw customers to you.

That's the idea of this book—how to get customers to come to you easily and without a lot of ongoing effort on your part. I want them knocking on your door so that all you have to do is open it and welcome them in!

I founded my last company with the intention of selling vegetable seeds. But I was unsure what to call it at first. I knew I was attracted to the idea of sustainability. This was back before it was in vogue. I also knew I liked the idea of being able to provide and grow your own food. THAT was what sustainable meant to me, so I bought SustainableSeedCo.com and the company was launched.

## BRANDING FUNDAMENTALS

Years later, when the idea of sustainability and growing your own food became popular, the fact that our name was "Sustainable" meant we were speaking directly to our customer in their language. We added so many customers simply by picking the right name—and talking their language.

Another reason we were successful was because of the searchability of the name—people wanted seeds that were sustainable. We were naturally the first listing to pop up.

We knew how valuable the right name could be. Years later we had the opportunity to buy another domain that would show up even better on Google than our own. It was like having a billboard in Times Square instead of in upstate New York. When we learned the price, we didn't hesitate—even though it was $3,000 because we knew it would get us lots of customers just because of the name!

This book is titled what it is for the same reason: Most coaches think they need leads and want a formula to follow. Hence, Coaching Leads Formula! But what most coaches don't yet realize (and this book is designed to educate about), is that you probably do have leads but just aren't following up with them or maintaining the conversation long enough for them to become clients.

Take a moment to consider your company and/or brand name. Keep in mind if you have a legal entity, your brand can still be something different. Although this is not legal advice (check with your attorney first), you may be able to operate under a DBA (doing business as).

What transformation does your client want? What words come to mind with it? Are you local to a specific area and, if so, can you have the area in the name?

If you get stuck or want inspiration, use a thesaurus and brain-storm using synonyms (I love that for figuring out variations of names), or even Google trends to see how much search volume that term will have.

## COACHING LEADS FORMULA

Likewise, in today's age of social media, it's important to brand yourself so that you have a consistent handle across the board. Ideally pick a social media name that can fit for all your social accounts. Since it's a crowded space on social media platforms, I suggest you do some research—finding one social handle will make connecting with you much easier.

If you're having a difficult time getting one single social media handle, consider a modifier. I've seen many additions to the beginning and/or end of a handle that make it totally unique. Once you do that, I'd suggest buying that domain as well so you can put something on that website (even if your website is totally different, you can always have it push the visitor over to your usual site). Here are some ideas using my name as an example:

- First or Last name - @TheoBill
- Add "the" in front - @theTheoBill
- Use initials - @TBill
- I am - @iamTheoBill
- Ask - @AskTheoBill
- Job Title - @CoachTheoBill
- Mr., Ms., Mrs. - @MrTheoBill

There are great tools out there to figure out what social media handles are available as well as ways to buy a domain and have some very easy web hosting.

Check the resources guide at the end of the book for more information on the tools I've used and recommend.

# 4. Your Marketing Plan

In many of my conversations with coaches, I'll hear some variation of, "I just want to get on calls," or "Just turn on the ads and let me get clients" or "I'll pay you a percentage if you get me clients." And that would be a fantastic outcome if it were possible. I don't want to say that it's impossible because ANYTHING is possible, but it's unlikely until you've done some work first.

Most coaches (and most business people) think they can throw an ad or a social media post out there and suddenly clients will be beating down their door to work with them.

That's not how it really works.

I hate to burst your bubble, but marketing takes work. I've seen so many coaches throw good money after bad ideas and I don't want you to be one of them. I urge you—don't waste advertising money until you understand the process.

This book is designed to help you with that. Let it be your guide in understanding the parts, pieces, and reasons for each element of a good marketing strategy that will make you money and get you those clients you're wanting.

I'm sure you've heard the analogy: Would you sleep with someone after just meeting them? Of course not. You build rapport, have conversation, test the chemistry, maybe go on a few dates, then possibly it gets to third base or beyond but it doesn't (usually) happen right after you first meet someone and simply say hello.

If you want to be a successful coach (which I sincerely want for you), you need to think of your marketing efforts as a conversation—one in which each stage has a desired outcome.

Let's go back to the dating analogy. If I went up to you and immediately asked for your phone number, you'd probably laugh or walk off. Hopefully you don't slap me! Seriously though, when I go up to you, my goal might be to get you to laugh—that's it. Once that stage is accomplished, I might consider trying for a phone number.

Coaches who fail will only think of their business (which you have now, if you hadn't thought of that before) as a simple one-stop shop. They think ads equal immediate coaching clients.

In reality, successful coaches know there's more to the equation than simply launching ads. If you learn what those pieces of the puzzle are, you're going to be head and shoulders above 90% of the rest of the coaches out there.

The two biggest pieces of the puzzle here are the stages of engagement and the elements of the Coaching Leads Formula.

## Engagement Cycle

In a nutshell, there are three stages of engagement in most prospect-client journeys:

1. **Know** - They're aware of YOU and/or your product. Eventually this merges into curiosity about you and your product or services. With that curiosity comes a need to identify people who are similar.

## YOUR MARKETING PLAN

2. **Like** - They like you and are convinced you *might* be able to help them through education and learning more about you, your services or products, and the clear, easy-to-follow path you lay out for them.

3. **Trust** - They are convinced you and your product are able to help them. Because you've let them go through the first two steps, it's easier to ask for their trust because you've earned it.

Once you understand that relationship cycle, you will be equipped to know how the pieces of the marketing plan fit together.

Your client needs to emotionally buy into the idea that you can help them. Trust has both an intellectual and emotional component. Remember, people make a buying decision first with their emotions, then they justify the emotions with the facts.

As I mentioned in the dating analogy, you want to have a few tiers of outcomes. First is awareness: They need to know about you before they decide to buy anything. Then during the dating process, you get to know one another, you build curiosity, you learn more about each other. Then eventually after they've decided they like you, they can take the leap of faith to trusting you.

Because you haven't rushed things and you've gotten to know them and let them know more about you and the way you work, you will have customers who love and rave about you. This will, in turn, make the sales conversation much easier, as it will happen naturally and in the time they need it to occur.

That is what your marketing plan and the email campaigns will do—they will educate and build rapport while building trust. We will go over the marketing plan and what goes into it in the following chapters. For now, just think of this as an overview.

# Coaching Leads Formula

Are you a math lover? In school, I certainly wasn't. I struggled with arithmetic and geometry. I REALLY struggled with Algebra I. Eventually in Algebra II, I had a teacher who was able to get through to me and suddenly I understood! It was like a new awareness and superpower was born within me. Suddenly I LOVED doing algebra—it all made sense (finally)! I was so excited by that moment that it changed my perception of math and formulas forever.

I've spoken to many coaches who have yet to figure out their marketing formula. They are frustrated and feel the idea of marketing and advertising to get clients is simply hopeless. They see other people doing it but don't think it can work for them. Well, I'm here to tell you—it's a science, not a mystical, magical potion you take.

Once you learn the basics and understand how things relate to each other, you'll be set. That's where the Coaching Leads Formula comes in. If you follow the steps, get the pieces in place, that frustration will evaporate and reveal a mountain of clients waiting to get your attention! With just six marketing assets, your business will begin to grow and eventually thrive.

# Marketing Assets

So, what are these marketing assets and why are they important?

The dictionary defines an asset as something of value. That's all a marketing asset is. It's something that not only is valuable in itself, but also in what it can do for you, which, in your case, is to bring you leads. In this book, we're talking about the various parts of your sales funnel, which we will talk about in greater depth later in the book.

I'll be 100% honest with you: You don't have to have a single marketing asset in order to be successful. All you really need is the willingness to talk to people. You need a sense of supreme curiosity. If you have a phone, you increase your reach.

## YOUR MARKETING PLAN

So why are marketing assets important? Without them you have to be extremely proactive and spend a lot of time talking to a lot of people in order to find clients.

You could get lucky—one coach I know specializes in smoking addiction. He goes to bars and restaurants and strikes up conversations with the smokers who are standing outside. He asks them if they still want to smoke or why they haven't quit yet. It's like fishing in a barrel—easy.

But for most of us, that's not quite the case. We don't have one super-specific place to find our ideal client. It often takes time and persistence because not every potential client is ready to become a client at the moment, we first meet them. So, we have to search those potential clients out wherever they are.

If you're anything like me, I'd prefer to be fishing in a barrel rather than an ocean! I'd rather they line up to ask me to help them than have to go out and hunt for them in the proverbial haystack.

If you are like me, then you will love what marketing assets can do for you!

As I mentioned before, the essence of marketing is simply having a communication with your prospect and building trust through the process.

Just like a good conversation, you want it to be as smooth and easy as possible. By including certain social cues (and by not omitting others), you can make a conversation go easier.

Think of your marketing materials (lead magnet, landing page, email sequence) as road signs on the highway—clear, to the point, and helpful.

If you're driving on the Autobahn in Germany, you can go really fast! Contrast that to a backcountry dirt road, and you can hardly go more than 20 miles an hour.

## COACHING LEADS FORMULA

Why the difference?

The cars and drivers might be the same, but the road is different. One is designed for speed. The foundations go nearly three feet deep and are engineered to have an uber-smooth driving surface with gentle bends and curves. The other is simply carved out of the raw earth with a tractor—full of rocks, bumps, and short sightlines. In a nutshell, there's lots of speed bumps!

In your marketing materials and the conversation you're having, you want to avoid as many speed bumps as possible.

Said another way, you want your prospects to always be nodding "yes" to you, building rapport. You never want them to be judging you and thinking "maybe not" for any reason.

Especially at first—you only get a tiny window to convince them to stick around. Even though you're not asking them for anything (like money or an email), you are, in fact, asking them for their attention and time.

Respect their attention, honor their time, and you'll be fine.

Remember, marketing is a conversation. So with each marketing asset you create, you need to be aware of where you are in the conversation. With each stage of the conversation, there are limits to the rapport and trust that you've built or earned. If you're aware of those limits and respect them, you will know what to say, when to say it, and how to say it.

Your primary assets are going to be your website/landing pages, your lead magnet, and your email list. We will be talking about each of those in upcoming chapters.

# YOUR MARKETING PLAN

## The Platinum Rule

We all know the "Golden Rule," which is, 'Treat others as you want to be treated.'

But in marketing, that doesn't go far enough. You have your history, your experiences, and your own unique internal representations of what things mean to YOU.

With marketing, we're concerned with how things mean to YOUR CLIENT.

Hence, the Platinum Rule was born, 'Treat others as THEY want to be treated.'

You might like Brussels sprouts, but your clients might hate them (personally I love them roasted with garlic and sea salt). If you ignore how your client will interpret things, you're going to lose them.

Keep that in mind, and you'll go far!

26

# 5. The CLF Recipe

In the old Disney cartoon film, Fantasia, there is a scene in which the sorcerer's apprentice (Mickey Mouse) is told to bring water in from the well and then the sorcerer goes to bed. After the sorcerer goes to bed, the apprentice dons the sorcerer's hat and enchants the broom to carry the water buckets instead, so he can take a nap - he delegated!

While the broom is carrying the water, Mickey falls asleep but eventually awakens to the broom overfilling the water trough and making a huge mess. The broom doesn't listen when Mickey tells it to stop, so Mickey makes a quick decision and tries to destroy the broom by chopping it up with an ax. Instead of destroying the broom, though, he creates multiple brooms like clones carrying water—lots of them, which makes the situation even worse!

Eventually the sorcerer awakens to a flood and quickly puts an end to it, finding a chastened Mickey Mouse wet and hiding under the spell book. Mickey gives him his hat back and starts to mop up, learning that there is no shortcut to magical power and wisdom.

By the way, if you didn't notice, that was a perfect hero's journey, which you will read more about in the upcoming chapter.

## COACHING LEADS FORMULA

Wouldn't it be wonderful to be able to make copies of yourself to help you (instead of making a mess, of course)? In your case, you don't need a wizard's hat, just a bit of technology to get what feels like multiple versions of you!

Even though you might not have a magic hat, you have something almost as good—computers! With them you can create wonderful assets that, once created, will magically go on doing their job even if you take a nap.

Through the magic of the computers and the internet, you can put systems in place. With those systems running smoothly, you will consistently improve the relationship with your prospect and build the rapport necessary for them to become a client, all without you having to lift another finger.

The MOST important thing is to consistently remain in your prospect's mind. Not all prospects are clients yet, but eventually, if you're persistent enough and set up the right systems, you will be the obvious choice once they reach the point they need help.

These systems are the basics of a marketing plan, otherwise known in the industry as a funnel. Now I know what you're thinking "I don't need a funnel! That's for someone else."

I've got news though. You DO need a funnel, and guess what? You already have one, even if you didn't know you did! If you have clients, you already have a funnel. If you're doing any kind of coaching (even if it's for free), you have a funnel!

A sales funnel is simply a systematic way to have lots of conversations going on all the time. They work 24/7 without you having to lift a finger. They're an ideal way to get consistent revenue.

## THE CLF RECIPE

Once you create this funnel and tweak it so that it's working, it can be your solution to everything you'd like. It is a better investment than anything you could put in the stock market, and it's a way to create customers on demand. When you get it dialed in, you will have a true business, not simply a hobby that makes you money.

You will still need to have one-on-one conversations with people. And you'll get to work with amazing clients, but the process of getting those clients will be easier and you'll have them lining up and knocking on your door.

Your current funnel might consist of going to a networking event and talking to people who might express an interest in your services. Perhaps then you have a call with them and they sign up with you on that call! Or it might be a friend of a friend who referred you to them and you had a call six months ago, but they never followed through and signed up.

Those are funnels. They're not very consistent and they require a lot of active participation by you, but they're still funnels.

My goal is to help you develop a funnel that doesn't take a lot of your time once it's set up and brings a consistent source of prospects who will become a reliable stream of income for you.

A funnel does a number of things that are essential if you're to have a successful coaching business. A funnel will:

1. nurture the relationship with prospects by keeping you constantly in their awareness (a.k.a. "Top of Mind");

2. build rapport with prospects;

3. give you actionable information about your prospects and customers;

4. qualify your leads so you don't waste time;

5. drive a consistent stream of prospects to you;

6. make the sales conversation MUCH easier;

## COACHING LEADS FORMULA

7. focus your efforts on your expertise and dream client;

8. generate referrals that might not have fit the dream client persona; and

9. create customers (a.k.a. make you money).

Funnels work because they take someone through the Know-Like-Trust process that I already covered in an earlier. But to reframe it as a funnel, the fundamental process is quite simple. First someone has to become aware of you—that you even exist (through a referral, an ad, social media post, or some other way). Then they need to learn to like you, meaning you have built a rapport with them demonstrating your authority and expertise. Finally they learn to trust you. In other words, they believe you can help them and they trust you enough to put their money down.

Think of the last time you purchased something online. You might have seen an advertisement for the product you were looking at *(Know)*. You viewed the product on the website and thought it was worth purchasing *(Like)*. You then purchased the product *(Trust)*.

See how simple that can be?

If you want to make money from farming (which I did in a previous life), you can plow the fields, plant seeds, harvest the crops each year and repeat in the spring. But what if you were to plant a seed and every year you were able to harvest crops from it without having to do anything more? If you think of a fruit tree, that's how it works. You plant the apple tree, let it grow, and every year you get apples!

The different pieces of your marketing funnel are that way too. They're assets that, once created, you don't have to do much with—but they bear fruit 24/7. The assets don't have to be fancy, but they are important to have. Here's the essential assets of your sales funnel:

1. Dream Client Identity

2. Conversion Hook (one-line to one-page versions)

# THE CLF RECIPE

3.  Landing/Sales Page

4.  Thank You Page

5.  Lead Magnet Asset (either free or paid)

6.  Email Sequence (to deliver the lead magnet and/or nurture the prospects and turn them into leads who eventually become customers)

The first step in creating these assets is to figure out which communication channel you want to use—one that you enjoy. We want you to be comfortable and happy creating these assets rather than stress you out because it's something you're not into.

There are three main types of assets:

- **Video** - using either live or prerecorded video if you feel comfortable on camera and enjoy expressing things visually.

- **Audio** - using your voice through podcasts or phone calls if you enjoy speaking and do so fluently but might not feel comfortable on camera.

- **Written** - perhaps you don't enjoy off-the-cuff remarks and prefer a well -thought-out, written communique? Then blogs, articles, or even social media posts might be best for you.

Whichever method of communication you decide upon doesn't matter—your dream client probably will prefer it as well!

You might be thinking you have to do all three methods. That's ideal but not necessary when you're getting started. In fact, just start on one communication method (video, audio, or written) and pursue it for at least three-to-six months, get the hang of it, give it a fair shot, and see not only whether you enjoy it but if you're good at it.

It'll take a while to become consistent with it, but after you develop the habit, you'll start to see what works and what doesn't. You'll also discover what your prospects respond to!

## COACHING LEADS FORMULA

In essence, by creating these assets, you're becoming your own publishing house. It allows you to remain in your client's awareness using the type of communication that comes most naturally to you and will connect you with your clients. It lets them be part of the process and know more about you—developing more and more rapport, educating (by delivering value), and building that trust with them.

You are going to use these skills of creating assets later in the process to create your lead magnet. That will be a way for you to connect with your dream client's most urgent need.

First we need to learn more about who that client is, and that's what's coming up in the next chapter!

# 6. Dream Client Identity

Before you get started selling your coaching, you need to define who you're selling your coaching to. There are many books, websites, courses, and articles devoted to finding the ideal avatar.

Personally, I don't like the term avatar because it's cold and represents a mask. It's also less useful (if you're just getting started) for you to be able to imagine the person who would be your ideal client. That's why I like to think of them as dream clients rather than ideal avatars.

Here's the thing that NONE of those books, websites, courses, and articles talk about: The ideal dream client doesn't really matter. It is only important—if you DON'T have one.

Said another way, you need to figure out who your dream client is and where they hang out. Otherwise you will be talking to everyone everywhere and getting nowhere. You also need to identify your niche, meaning the market segment you are going to focus on.

What truly matters is for you to start the conversations. Until you have had consistent income and clients for a period of time, you can't begin to analyze what is similar, what worked, or what didn't work.

## COACHING LEADS FORMULA

If you've already been in business for a while, you could comb through the data of your existing clients to find who your current customer demographic is and what their psychographic is, but even then you might be working with clients who are NOT your ideal clients. That is why this process can still apply to you.

When you think of the person you'd like to work with, what comes to mind? Since this is an exercise, go all out. Dream big!

Imagine the ideal person you'd LOVE to work with—the type of person who you get excited to help. How can your unique specialty or gift help them to unlock *their* unique challenges and, in turn, convert them into raving fans?

You might be thinking, "Wait. If I get specific, won't I be limiting my possible client base? Won't it make some of them get turned off?" Yes, some will be turned away, not because you said something but more because they simply weren't a fit.

Don't get caught in the trap of worrying about what might happen in the future. Your clients in six months will be different from the ones you have today. Your clients in six years will be different from those in a year from now because YOU will be a different person with different expertise and interests and so you will attract a different clientele.

The beauty of the coaching industry is that you have access to the entire world now because of the internet and Zoom. This allows you to pick EXACTLY who you want to work with! It ALSO allows you to discover how to set yourself apart from the pack, how to be the lone wolf, how to find your Blue Ocean.

The Blue Ocean strategy was coined by W. Chan Kim & Renée Mauborgne when they were trying to explain the idea that companies and industries who are in existence already live in a red ocean where lots of predators are already eating...hence the "red," a.k.a. blood in the water. The idea is to find *your* Blue Ocean where you can be the top predator who doesn't have a lot of competition.

The best way to distinguish yourself is by being yourself. Use your unique interests, quirks, and methods of working. By being yourself and finding *your* Blue Ocean, you'll also start to become your client's obvious choice to help solve their problems or challenges. You will make it easy for them to find you. That will set you apart from the rest of the other coaches!

As an example, I love being outdoors and hiking, which often comes out in my writing. I know not everyone loves the outdoors, but this is me—and I know it'll draw my dream clients to me because I choose to share it.

# Target Niche

Step one is finding the niche you want to work in. From a very broad sense you can coach almost any niche, but if you want to be profitable you will want to focus your coaching on one of three main markets:

- Health

- Wealth

- Relationships

Even if you're a health coach, don't feel limited to *just* health—you can still focus on the financial or relationship problems that arise from living an unhealthy lifestyle. Don't box yourself strictly into health, although with any additional sub-areas, it'll *probably* be in a sub-niche of the health market.

Finding a niche is important because it allows you to find your blue area of the ocean easier. You want to get specific enough so you can stand out from the crowd. Instead of targeting people interested in just health, you might want to niche further down.

COACHING LEADS FORMULA

Lets say your target audience is mothers. Well, then it's moms who are interested in getting healthy. But how can you niche down further? Perhaps they want to get healthy because they just gave birth and want to get rid of the baby weight. Maybe it's because they want to return to work and want the extra energy they'll need. That's a pretty specific niche! We've gone from just health to women who have just given birth who want to (not just get healthy) but lose their baby weight and regain energy because they want to return to the workforce!

Did you see what that last part did as well? It added a complementary macro-niche. The wealth niche! Now you're not only talking about health, you're also talking about their career and how they can support and provide for their family. Look for opportunities where your niches can overlap the big macro-niches.

You can see how there might be a lot of coaches talking about health but probably not that many speaking directly to moms who just gave birth and want to drop those extra pounds to get their summer bikini body back and have the energy and inspiration to get back in the workforce.

In the next step you'll learn how to figure out not only what the niche is, but the details of your dream client's life and needs.

## Client Identity

Step two is figuring out the person. You've already laid the groundwork on the market niche you will be addressing, but now let's single out your person in that crowd of potential prospects.

This is the foundation of why it's critical to pick SOMEone to direct your conversation (a.k.a. marketing) toward. If you're speaking to everyone then you're going to be lost in the sea of choices. But if you're speaking to a specific person, THEN you will be able to make a connection that verifies you are their ONE.

# DREAM CLIENT IDENTITY

You could get lucky—some coaches do! They might be the perfect combination of social butterfly and charming savvy entrepreneur (with a big dash of luck). If that's you, more power to you, friend! But many of us need to speak to a specific person and swim away from the red ocean to find our calm seas where we are the obvious choice.

Highlight your unique gifts rather than subdue them. Celebrate your weirdness! Be the big nerd or fitness fanatic. Don't be shy about it, because someone will say, "Wow, they get me!" What hobbies, interests, or specialties do you have that will set you apart? Clients won't choose you because you're the SAME as the other coaches…they'll choose you because you are DIFFERENT from the other coaches.

Being like everyone else is, well, boring…and we all know it's the squeaky wheel that gets the oil! It's why I don't believe in true competition within the coaching world—because personality determines the relationship so much. You can try and be like all the others but, in reality, nobody has the exact same experiences or ways of communicating.

Each coach has a unique process as well. You will find your clients because you are YOU. The more authentically and courageously you share the beauty and uniqueness that is you, the easier you will make it for your clients to find you.

Figuring out who your dream client is will unlock so much information that is crucial to the rest of the process. This process will give you a lot of the information you will need for your landing page, your lead magnet, and your email sequences, which will be discussed in future chapters.

This is how you can be effective as well as cost-effective, so do these exercises to the best of your ability. We're going to look at our dream client from two perspectives: demographics and psychographics.

## COACHING LEADS FORMULA

**Demographics:** More objective ways of describing the person; more numbers driven. What is their zip code, income, how many (if any) children, what age, etc.

**Psychographics:** More subjective description of the dream client. What drives them? What hobbies do they enjoy? Why do they love (or hate) their work? What do they think about, focus on, and show interest in?

Because demographics are more about the numbers, they can be sort of dry but they're still important. Demographics can give you the edge, which makes a marketing campaign thrive or fail. Get it right and you've got an easy job; get it wrong and you'll be working much harder. Always be aware that if you're talking to a married person, you're going to say things differently than if they were single. Keep in mind whether they have kids or not—or even if the kids are toddlers or are in high school.

## DREAM CLIENT IDENTITY

**Exercise:** What are the basic demographics of your avatar—age, gender, location, income, etc.?

_____

_____

_____

_____

_____

_____

_____

When you're thinking about how to describe your dream client, get as detailed as possible. I like to have my coaches describe _in detail_ a day in the life of their dream client. Start off from waking up, their morning routine, then work, what they do, who they interact with, all the way through their nighttime routine and what they read or watch before bed.

Once you've done that, go back and try to infer their values, what they are interested in, and their point of view on things.

After discovering the demographic of your dream client—the numbers stuff—it's time for the things of the imagination: What are their dreams, desires, despairs, and dilemmas? As a coach I'm sure you know about toward versus away from motivation and the power both have. We're going to examine both sides of that but also in two different timelines—present versus future.

# COACHING LEADS FORMULA

**Pro Tip:** If you have clients or are having sales/discovery conversations already, you're ahead of the game. I hope you take notes during these calls because, if you do, you can refresh your memory on the exact turns of phrase your prospects have used.

Remember—be as detailed and specific as possible. If you already have clients, use them and their EXACT language, word for word.

**Desires (toward present):** What things do they want? What kind of goals do they have? What do they want right now that would make their life better? How could their life be better in the short-term—tomorrow, next week, next month? What would be different in their life that will prove to them their dreams will come true?

---

**Exercise:** What desires right now (or shortly) do your clients want? Be specific—how could their life be easier in the present moment?

_____

_____

_____

_____

_____

_____

_____

# DREAM CLIENT IDENTITY

**Dilemmas (away from present):** What is preventing them from having their ideal life? What is causing them pain right now? What is holding them back every day?

**Exercise:** What dilemmas in the present does your client experience? What happens every single day that frustrates them?

_____

_____

_____

_____

_____

_____

**Dreams (toward future):** What do they want their life to look like in the future? Who do they want to have in that life with them? How will they feel? Who will they become once they have that dream? This part is more long-term. Think six months to ten years. This is often the strongest source of motivation for them and can be incredibly powerful!

**Exercise:** What dreams in the future do your clients want? Be specific and think long-term—in one, five, ten years, what will they be/do/have?

_____

_____

_____

_____

_____

_____

## COACHING LEADS FORMULA

**Despairs (away from future):** What do they fear? What will happen in their life if nothing changes? Will things get worse? What could happen if they do? What fears are holding them back from moving forward? What are the top three things they are terrified will happen? What keeps them awake at night?

**Exercise:** What despairs in the future do your clients want to avoid? Be specific and think long-term - in one, five, ten years, what will they lose out on? Who won't be in their life anymore?

_____

_____

_____

_____

_____

_____

_____

_____

An important aspect of your dream client is understanding what might be preventing them from engaging with you. I know this sounds like mind-reading, but I want you to try to think of everything that might prevent them from working with you. You need to know this so you can address it and preempt their objection before they bring it up.

## DREAM CLIENT IDENTITY

**Exercise:** What do you think your dream client's biggest objections might be to working with you or investing in your coaching?

_____

_____

_____

_____

_____

_____

_____

_____

Once you've figured out these things, you'll be able to understand your dream client and start talking to them and addressing their needs, dreams, and fears!

That's not the end of the story though. Next up, you want to figure out where they are in their thinking. Do they know what their REAL problem is yet?

Ask yourself: What do THEY think will solve their problem? What magic pill could they take and make everything work the way they want?

# COACHING LEADS FORMULA

**Exercise:** What does your dream client think is their problem?

_____

_____

_____

_____

_____

_____

_____

_____

Now that you know how they think their problems can be solved, what do YOU think they need? We're figuring out the gap here between what they think the problem is and what the problem really is.

Probably the most powerful question you could help them with is what is at stake for them—what will happen in their life if they don't engage with you and get your coaching. How will their life be in six months, a year, five years? Be specific and use your imagination. Think of all the aspects of their life and, based on your experience, try to come up with the absolute worst-case scenario possible.

## DREAM CLIENT IDENTITY

**Exercise:** What is the cost of inaction for your dream client? What does their life look like in the future and who is (or isn't) a part of their life at this time?

_____

_____

_____

_____

_____

_____

_____

_____

By applying these questions, you're going to learn exactly how to talk to your dream client and, in the process, you will become the obvious choice to help them solve their challenges. Before we finish this exercise though, it's always good to imagine what they've tried before to solve the issues they have. Why hasn't THAT solution worked? What products or processes have they tried before? And what about those solutions frustrated them?

# COACHING LEADS FORMULA

**Exercise:** What has your dream client tried in the past that hasn't worked out the way they wanted? What have they failed at before meeting you?

# 7. Conversation Hook

With all the information you've gathered on your dream client, now you're prepared to create your conversation hook! Sometimes called your elevator pitch, your one-liner or, in Hollywood, a logline. This statement is how you 'call in' your clients and have them know you truly *see and understand* them.

With the exception of knowing who your client is, this is the most powerful piece of the puzzle because all else falls in line behind it. This is the keystone that you will build your marketing systems around.

As a coach, you know how much value words can carry—when they're spoken to ourselves and also to others. With each word we utter we create our reality.

We assign meanings and then values based on words. Why would you take orders to go marching into battle just because someone has a title of President if the word didn't carry meaning? Getting this statement right can truly make or break your business, so let's dive into it!

It's a simple framework that is meant to describe what your product or service does. It creates curiosity. It begins the conversation and allows the prospect to say, "Really, tell me more!"

## COACHING LEADS FORMULA

It's basically **who** you help, **what** problem you're helping them solve, the **dreams** they will have or become, and *ideally* have it be in a specified **time frame**.

I know a timeline is impossible to predict with some coaching outcomes. But if you can put a time frame onto some aspect of the goal, it makes for a very tangible metric by which the client can judge your results. So make it a very attainable goal. And make it highly specific so we can say "Yes, we got this," or "Not yet, keep going."

With the Dream Client Identity exercises, you learned what problems they're facing and what they call themselves (what they consider their identity to be).

You already know at least one or two of your dream client's biggest problems and exactly how they describe them. Now I want you to pick one of those problems and start playing around with it by reframing the problem in the form of a question. (Jeopardy anyone? LOL). You could start it by asking, "Have you ever…" or "You know how… ."

Why a question instead of a statement? The question form, especially the open form, draws someone in. Their subconscious knows they need to pay attention. The question engages them and piques their curiosity and gets them agreeing with you immediately.

By starting off with a question that touches on one of their problems, you're also hooking them into your world and, by entering into the conversation already going on in their head, you will become the obvious choice to help them resolve that problem. Your question demonstrates that you have a clear understanding of their problem, and your dream client will be instantly intrigued because you've immediately demonstrated what's in it for them.

# CONVERSATION HOOK

If you ever have listened to a good Ted talk, many of the speakers start their talk with a question because it hooks the audience and gets them instantly engaged. Traditionally, many conversation hooks are framed in the form of a statement. BUT, when you're talking to someone in a statement, they often are thinking about what they're going to say in response rather than listening to what you're actually saying. With a question, you engage the curiosity element of their brain, and they pay attention.

Don't get too complicated here. Keep it simple. Your dream client's biggest problem is the best one to start with, but at most include the top two as your focus in the statement. Obviously, it goes without saying that the problem(s) should be what your coaching will be able to solve or resolve.

---

**Exercise:** Who is your dream client and what is the problem your coaching helps them to solve? For example: *Most coaches don't make enough money to support themselves through their coaching.*

## COACHING LEADS FORMULA

The next step is the solution. How does your coaching solve their problem(s)? What will they get to be, do, or have as a result of your coaching? Remember this is meant to illustrate to them what the value of your solution is meant to represent. You've already hooked them by introducing the problem that relates directly to their life— now you're going to be introducing the solution!

When you're talking about the solution, make sure it's linked directly to the problem. That means don't talk about a really tangible problem then go to a really high-level solution. Make the solution specifically applicable and something they can see, hear, or feel directly.

The solution part is more about their immediate desires—the short-term goals they want to accomplish or achieve. It's tempting to immediately talk about their big dreams, but at the moment they haven't gotten the frustrations of the present out of the way, so keep it focused on the short-term and stay as specific as you can.

Many coaches I've worked with like to go on and hit every single thing—they get really complicated in their statements. Don't go down that road. - As Da Vinci said, simplicity is better. The sales adage "When you confuse, you lose" applies here. Keep it directly in relation to the benefit or dream they get as a result of your coaching. You have about four-to-six seconds of brain time before their attention starts to wander. Keep things clear, simple, and short.

One way to think of this is: How would you describe it to a six-year-old? If you can't do that, then you need to simplify it.

But don't forget to weave in your business name so they have it linked in their minds to the solution!

CONVERSATION HOOK

## Exercise: What is the solution your coaching provides?

For example: *By using the Client Leads Formula, they will learn how to make consistent income.*

_____

_____

_____

_____

_____

_____

Finally we're into the home stretch. This last part is about their dreams. How will their life be better because of your coaching solution?

Remember to keep it tangible. If you're describing it, you want to be able to see or hear or touch it. This will be the best part of the statement that will really pull folks to you. This is what they want in their heart of hearts, and because YOU are the one to put it so clearly, it will create an undeniable bond between you and them.

If you're able to, it's wonderful to delineate a time frame here. As a coach, you already know that "the presenting problem isn't really the problem." Meaning, there's almost always deeper work to be done. But for this part of the relationship, you're only dealing with the tip of the iceberg here—so if you can promise a time-based solution, go for it!

When you're making the statement, speak in 'you' terms. This should be 100% about them, not you. Again, keep it as short and sweet as possible. Remember the KISS principle.

COACHING LEADS FORMULA

**Exercise**

What is the dream outcome for your client they will get after working with you?

For example: *In six weeks, you will learn the tools that let you focus on the areas of your life you'd sacrificed and had given up on.*

_____

_____

_____

_____

_____

_____

_____

_____

Let's put it all together now. Take each part of that process and create your full conversation hook. It's natural to have it go long, and that's okay. This isn't a hard-and-fast framework. You want it to sound natural, so you may need to change it up some as you refine it. But try and keep it as short as you can; it needs to sound natural. You know the idea here, so just go with it.

# CONVERSATION HOOK

**Exercise:** What is the full conversation hook?

For example: *You know how most coaches don't make enough money through their coaching? With Client Leads Formula, in just six weeks, they learn how to make consistent income so they can focus on the areas of life they'd given up on.*

_____

_____

_____

_____

_____

_____

_____

_____

Once you have created this conversation hook, practice it. As Zig Ziglar says, "Repetition is the mother of learning..." or as they said in the days of Caesar, "Repetitio est mater studiorum." Say it to yourself over and over like Cameron did in *Ferris Bueller's Day Off*. Say it in the shower when you're rinsing off the shampoo. Say it to your dog or cat. Practice it and work it so you can say it quickly and easily. It not only needs to be believable but sound natural.

# COACHING LEADS FORMULA

Once you've practiced saying it in private, start saying it in public. Say it on your social media videos, at networking events, when you're out with friends. Say it everywhere you can. By saying it, you're going to make people curious. They will want to know more about you and what/how you work.

Ideas of where and how to use your conversation hook:

- Social media bios
- Business card
- Email tagline
- On your website - Home page and About Us pages

The beauty of this process is that it will not only attract your dream clients, it will also often repel the type of client you don't want. They will hear what you're saying and know that you are NOT for them!

It's just as important to know who you're avoiding as it is who you want to attract, because those people you can't or don't want to help will be a huge time and resource sink into which you pour your heart, soul, and money and never see a return. Those are NOT clients. They will sap your motivation, strength, and joy. It's okay to say they're not a fit, because there will be another coach who can help them and is better equipped for that challenge than you.

# 8. Your Hero's Journey

Now that you've found who your dream client is, you can start to pull them into your world. The next step is to build massive amounts of rapport, and the best, fastest, and easiest way is through your story.

Stories are powerful. In fact, they're the most powerful way to communicate. It's why we've passed down stories from one generation to the next. Stories can inspire or divide; they can lead to transformation and growth. You can open locked doors or forge an instant bond through a powerful story.

We humans have told stories since we first began to talk. I'd wager they are burned into our genetics. The most persuasive people are also the best storytellers—because a good story can not only get an idea across, but it can also knock down barriers with the irresistible force of a tsunami.

There are about seven basic plots for a story, and once you know the basics of the story, you'll be able to know the plot of any movie, book, or play in about five minutes. However, you don't need to learn all seven plots.

## COACHING LEADS FORMULA

The simplest way to craft your story is by using the template of the hero's journey. There can be a number of steps, but I'd like to distill the most essential parts of the story so you can create your own hero's journey story easily and quickly. It comes down to three sections that revolve around the rock bottom moment.

**Before:** What was your life like before you hit rock bottom? What was the old life like? Was it good, bad, or in between? What is ordinary life like? What is your hero's basic nature? His skills and his latent superpowers? Somewhere in this part, we meet the guide, the person who shows the hero where/what to go/do. This is essentially your role in their journey.

When you're telling this story, you want to use your journey to illustrate you've been there and done that. But you want to keep your dream client engaged. Phrase the story in terms of them, not you. Instead of saying, "I was walking into the cave," say, "Imagine walking into the cave." Invite them to take part in the story.

**During:** This is the rock-bottom moment. But you also need to describe the events that led up to it. What struggles (often many) did you undergo that led you here? What did you face? Who were the enemies of this story? Here you need to get *really* vulnerable and share your deepest, darkest fears, suspicions, and failures. Without this honesty and vulnerability, you won't be able to connect with your audience. Talk about the moment of transformation and revelation—what did you learn that you had never thought of or felt (about yourself or others)?

**After:** Once you've passed through the ordeal of the transformation, how does life look now? What is possible that wasn't before the journey? How do you feel? What new insights do you see that were hidden before? What is your new normal?

## YOUR HERO'S JOURNEY

Our job as coaches is to hold the door of possibility open for our clients when they think it's shut to them. It's our job to inspire them to step through that door into a new reality full of possibility and hope. Stories are powerful tools you can use to illustrate and inspire such transformation.

I love to refer to *The Lord of the Rings* because it's the perfect hero's journey, but you can also look at the story of Sylvester Stallone and how *Rocky* came to be filmed. Or the story of *Star Wars* (the original movie). All of them follow the arc of a hero and their life before, the challenges they faced, the moment of transformation, and suddenly a new (better), normal life.

Once you learn how to connect through stories, you will be able to create instant rapport and interest. Good storytelling takes practice, but once you get there and recognize the power, you'll never go back.

By sharing your story you're going to build a connection with your prospects. You want them to feel as if you're telling THEIR story as well as your own.

When you're first beginning to tell your story, it's challenging to remember it's in the past for you, but it's in your client's present. At this point in your life you have a nuanced, experienced way of talking about your past. You might even use industry-specific jargon, but do your best to speak as plainly and simply as possible. Try to keep the technical terms for once they've become a client or are further down your funnel.

Remember how things felt, seemed, looked, and sounded when you were FIRST going through this challenge? Your client is there NOW, so use language and phrases they will understand. Instead of saying, "I know my obesity is a challenge," try "I hate being so fat." I know it's not an empowering statement, but you want to mirror your client's exact phrasing and language.

# COACHING LEADS FORMULA

Later on you can teach them about talking to themselves in a more empowering way. Another example might be, "That man gave me an opportunity to reflect on myself," but your client might say, "He pissed me off by calling me stupid!" Do you see the difference?

It's easy and probably second nature by now to use the language, skills, and tools you've acquired in the process of building rapport. But the ironic thing is that expertise will set you apart from them. Instead of creating a connection, it cements the DISconnection.

You want your client to IMMEDIATELY say, "That's me—they totally understand me!" The way to do that is to speak their language. Use their phrases and words when crafting your story. Exactly—word for word if possible.

Resist the urge to use big, professional words when crafting your hero's journey even if you have difficult topics that you think ABSOLUTELY need big, professional words. If you MUST, then use an analogy: say it's "sort of like…" and insert a very simple-to-understand analogy. For example, I recommended to a friend that he get evaluated for a stem-cell procedure to repair his compressed spinal issues rather than having his vertebrae fused (which is a life-altering procedure). Instead of going into the details (mostly because I'm not the expert), I told him, "They teach your own body to heal itself." That avoided the specifics but got the point across and was easy to understand.

Another thing you want to be sure to do is to use sensory language. By painting the sensory picture of what happened, you're going to draw the listener into your story and help them identify with your main character. So make sure to vividly describe how things looked, sounded, felt, and maybe even describe the smell and taste if it's appropriate. The more sensory description you include, the more your prospect will be pulled into your story and the more easily you are going to get your point across.

# YOUR HERO'S JOURNEY

## Exercise: Before, During, After

### BEFORE

What was leading up to your rock-bottom moment? What was your life like? How were you feeling? What challenges (if any) were you facing? This was your old normal. Often in this period there is a feeling of aimlessness or low-level unease. Some folks say they feel like everything was fine (a.k.a. bored but nothing bad happened) until some big event happened that started the downward spiral.

# COACHING LEADS FORMULA

## DURING

Life has suddenly changed. Now the challenges that were minor before have become insurmountable. Now you're unsure if life will ever be like it was. You probably face a series of small challenges that lead further and further down toward the pit until you finally reach rock bottom. Describe those series of events and the moment that you hit your deepest, darkest moment of the soul.

_____

_____

_____

_____

_____

_____

_____

_____

_____

_____

_____

_____

_____

YOUR HERO'S JOURNEY

## AFTER

After you had the rock-bottom moment, you probably realized something new—you had an epiphany where life had a different outlook. Suddenly things seemed new, fresh, and possible. Little by little life began to get better and, in fact, it's even better now than it ever has been. Talk about that process of becoming the new version of yourself.

_____

_____

_____

_____

_____

_____

_____

_____

_____

You'll want to have a couple different versions of this. Create a short, one- or two-minute version, a longer five-minute version, and perhaps a ten-minute version. When you're just getting started, focus on the five-minute version because there you won't be constrained by time. Once you've practiced it a bit, you'll know the essential parts to keep in for your one-minute version as well as thoughts on how to expand on the story for your ten-minute version.

## COACHING LEADS FORMULA

When you're telling your story, make sure to use all the senses—put your audience in your shoes. Paint the picture fully. Immerse them into what you were seeing, hearing, feeling, smelling, and tasting.

Once you have developed that story, practice it. Just like your conversation hook, your story needs to be believable and come easily without effort. Tell it to the mirror, record yourself doing it on video until it becomes second nature. Then start to share it in public like you did your conversation hook: through networking events, social media posts, or interviews. It's the key to unlocking your business success!

WEBSITE

# 9. Website

I've already mentioned the way Mickey cloned the broomsticks. This is how we clone YOU. A website is another arrow in your quiver that will allow you to minimize your time involved in the process of converting a cold lead to a sales call or paid client.

I'll say right off the bat—you don't have to have a website, but if you want your customers lining up, begging you to say yes, then you will need a website and the accompanying domain name.

A website doesn't have to be complicated or fancy to be effective. In fact, a simple, tasteful site that introduces you to your clients, I think, is better than a complicated and distracting one. You will want to answer a few questions, build your authority, and hopefully remove some objections.

Don't get too caught up on building the website. There are people out there who specialize in building websites and some are quite affordable and talented. What you need to concern yourself with is what will be on the website—the text, the basic images, the basic layout.

A good website can be worth millions of dollars. So many coaches have websites that aren't worth anything because they're not using good, sound marketing practices or following best practices.

COACHING LEADS FORMULA

Remember I told you how I came across my website name and because of it, we got a lot of customers JUST because we chose the right name?

Well, I also learned there are things you want to have on a website and things to avoid.

The basics you want on your website are:

- **Home Page:** This is how you say, "Hello, come on in!" to your prospect. Address them by name, occupation, or challenge directly. Include some attractive graphics of smiling, happy people that could be your ideal client. Speak to their challenge and tell them they've found their solution!

- **About Us Page:** On this page you get to talk about your journey a bit and build further rapport. Your transformation journey would be a good thing to include here, but remember—keep the page about them and don't make it all about you. Invite them into the story by asking them questions, identifying with their pains and dreams. "I wonder if you've experienced XYZ," or "I'll bet you've had those same feelings." There's lots of ways to include them in the story— get creative!

- **Services Page:** Outline a few services you offer. I suggest keeping it very simple and don't go into a huge amount of detail. Talk about the benefits they will get and the transformation they will have by working with you. I wouldn't include price here—that should be a discussion you have with them directly.

- **Contact Page:** Ideally you want to include the top ways they can get in touch with you. I'd include your social media, a calendar booking form to schedule a call with you, and a form that they can complete to send an email to you directly.

Remember, a website doesn't have to be complicated. It can even be **one single page** with sections instead of pages.

64

## WEBSITE

However, there are some things you want to make sure you're watching out for, because they are going to make your site much better and useful to you as a business owner.

1. **Simple** - Keep the design easy on the eyes. You want it to look attractive and uncluttered. Limit the colors and use them judiciously. You'll want to have one or two dominant colors and another that is for your calls to action. Also, stay with two font faces—you don't want to have fifteen different fonts and colors.

2. **Call to Action** - Ensure prospects click on your calls to action by being direct. Don't tell them to "learn more" when you mean "Book Your Call TODAY." Have it be strong, direct, and actionable. Assume they're going to do what you want.

3. **Whitespace** - In order to appreciate the text and images, you need to have whitespace (empty space). When you use empty space well, you can direct the viewer's attention to what is really important. With too much crowded text, the viewer can't distinguish what is important and what is not.

4. **Sign-up form** - You want to have a sign-up form on every page of your website so you don't miss an opportunity for them to sign up for your lead magnet. Also, it's good to have a pop-up when someone leaves the website. I know it's annoying, but in the end it works! Period.

5. **Page load times** - Most of the world has fast internet. We are wired to expect websites to show up instantly. The longer your page takes to load, the more people are going to click away. This means keep your pages lean and light. It also means using images sparingly, and please no slideshows. Slideshows bulk up the page size and they're often very user UNfriendly.

6. **Mobile-friendly** - A huge percentage of traffic will be from people on their phones, so make sure the page loads easily and looks good on the phone.

## COACHING LEADS FORMULA

7. **Test** - Have everyone you know look at the site on their computers and phones. If there's a problem, ask them to take a picture or a screen capture of it so you can address and fix it (or tell your web designer to do that).

8. **Tracking links** - Every website has a cookie nowadays. They're used for many purposes, but you want to be able to track prospects and have the ability to retarget them on Facebook and/or Google. If you don't have cookies installed, you're missing out on a HUGE opportunity to continue the conversation with your prospects.

# 10. Landing Page

The previous chapter covered the basic pages you will want on your website. A landing page is separate from a webpage though. Websites encompass many different topics. Landing pages are designed to direct the prospect to one specific goal. One route they can take. In general, a website needs to have certain elements, but a landing page is more focused.

The purpose of a landing page is to direct your visitor to a specific purpose and outcome. We're going to discuss this as if it were a stand-alone, single page, which it is. It's not a website. A website has multiple pages, and you can click around and look at different pages with different purposes. A landing page only has a series of content blocks—without the menu, side bar, etc. Remember, we want to get laser-focused on converting those visitors into eventual customers!

Recall how we talked about the power of words and how they can influence us and create meaning. You learned about the power of marketing over branding. By focusing on the marketing of your landing page first and the branding second, your page will be far more effective because the sole purpose of your landing page is to get clients.

A landing page helps to increase the rapport with your prospective clients, steer non-clients away, and smooth the transition with visitors as they go from prospect to client.

# COACHING LEADS FORMULA

Obviously, you need to use words to sell your idea. You've already learned about your client's dreams, desires, despairs, and dreads. You've created your conversation hook about who you help and how you help them achieve their goals. Now you get to use that to turn your landing page into a conversion machine.

When starting with a website or landing page, you want to start with the words, not the colors, fonts, or pictures. And most importantly, do not write a long, elaborate bio. Just like in the conversation hook, you want to be clear, concise, and persuasive. Speak to the problem they're having, your solution, and their goals and dreams.

Here are the basics of what needs to be on a landing page.

1. **The hero section** - This includes the BIG PROMISE and a call to action. You want to use as few words as possible. It's the big transformation you're selling. If necessary you can include a sub-header that explains a bit more but also calls out your client directly.

2. **The consequences** - What pains they are going through right now, and what pains will continue (and/or get worse) if they do nothing.

3. **The benefits** - This is the solution they're desperately seeking.

4. **The map** - How you are going to get the client from where they are to where they want to be.

5. **The reinforcement** - You can use the long version of your conversation hook here and go into more detail of the problems, the solutions, the goals, and the timelines they can expect.

6. **Authority statement** - Here is where you can include a little bit about your own journey and story. The purpose here is to prove that you know exactly what they're going through and, as a result, have the authority and compassion to help them on their journey.

LANDING PAGE

7. **Video** - A way to introduce yourself and restate much of what is in the text but in a more interactive way.

We'll go into each of these elements in detail in a moment. But first, know that the order doesn't really matter *except* that the hero section MUST be first. And you don't need all of them either, but I'd suggest you have one through five. These elements, when done well, will create a compelling page that will persuade your prospects into becoming a lead, if not a customer, as a result.

I'm pretty confident after reading the sections below you'll have all you need for creating your own totally unique and successful landing page because by now, you have more marketing chops than most of the professional marketers out there!

# Hero Section

This is your opportunity to really hook your visitor and get them to stay on the page. This is the first thing your visitor will see when coming to your page. There was a study done in 2006 that said you have 0.05 seconds before a visitor will form an opinion on your website. You have to connect with them FAST, so make it good!

There are three elements to the hero section—the headline, the call to action, and the image. Your headline is arguably the most important. You have 6-12 words to convince your visitor to stay on the page and discover more about you and your coaching.

You want the headline to talk about your coaching and how it can make your client's life better. That's it. Simple, right? In concept yes, but in execution, more challenging.

Your headline needs to emphasize the transformation that your coaching will provide. It needs to describe your offer as well. It needs to be short, concise, and easy to understand. Does it pass the five-year-old test (when you tell it to a five-year-old, do they understand it)?

# COACHING LEADS FORMULA

## Exercise: What is your headline?

For example: Drop the weight and get your life back. Repair your relationship and find the love again. Seven steps to becoming a confident speaker. Learn the formula to create reliable income from your coaching business.

_____

_____

_____

_____

_____

_____

_____

A sub-headline is used when you need to expand or clarify on the headline. Use it to directly call out your client by name, job, or identity. You want it to reinforce the headline and still reference the transformation.

Keep in mind that you want to be as clear and concise as you can be. You don't want to confuse your visitors. You want to invite curiosity while hooking them by convincing them that you understand and know their pain.

# LANDING PAGE

In your call to action, you want to use action words. It's a call to ACTION (CTA), not a call to be passive. "Learn more" or "Find out more" are not telling your visitor to do anything. Be bold and lead them where you want them to go. Tell them specifically what you want them to do: "Book Your Call", "Sign Up Today," or even "Register Now" all are specific actions for them to take. If you confuse, you lose.

Last but not least is the image of your hero section. I believe in using an image rather than a video background simply because video takes much longer for the viewer to download. Remember, you want your page to be easy and simple to read but fast to load as well. Choose one image (no sliding carousels) that describes the transformation your coaching offers. If you are in doubt, pick an image that shows the happiness, joy, or satisfaction that your coaching will provide—show a happy person, smiling maybe with family, friends, or celebrating.

Most people reading this will scan the page in an F pattern—top left to right, then lower left across to right. For the layout, you want it to be simple and clear. In the top left is your logo, top right your call to action (CTA), then on the mid part of the F is the headline, below it the sub-headline, and directly below that is the call to action (repeated—give it love). Below the "fold," which refers to newspaper days when pages were folded in half, you can put the various benefits and features.

Here's a rough sketch. It's not meant to be anything more than an example to give you a visual so that you can focus on the important elements. Once you get these important parts of the equation right, you can then deliver them to your designer.

A good idea for the headline is to brainstorm. Write down as many as you can think of and then narrow it down to the top ten, then the top three, and test those to see which grabs people's attention best. Ask friends, colleagues, people at the gym, whoever you run into wherever you go. Once you get the hero's section done, you have gotten the biggest piece of your website done! Truly—this is the MOST important part of the process.

COACHING LEADS FORMULA

Congratulate yourself for a job well done!

## Consequences

You've already done a lot of work for this part when you created your Dream Client Identity. This section is so you can speak to the consequence of not engaging in your coaching.

I know it doesn't always feel good to emphasize the negative, but it's crucial that you provide contrast to the benefits.

You've been there and experienced the consequences of doing nothing—you know how miserable life can be. It's important to share that with the prospect so that they realize there IS a cost to inaction. You don't have to go on and on, but it's important that you remind them of what they already know in their hearts.

As a coach, we get paid to push. It is our job to hold the door open to our client's greatness. Some of them will naturally walk right through but many will need some motivation to, reluctantly at first, step through that doorway. We, as human beings, are often more motivated to avoid pain than to seek pleasure. It's part of our prehistoric brain telling us that change might result in something worse. You've got to show them that, without a doubt, doing NOTHING is even worse than staying the same.

A good deal of the marketing process is like painting a picture and then framing it. It's framing things in the best way to achieve our intended outcome, which is the client's success.

When we talked about the website earlier, I mentioned using white space and how it creates contrast to focus the viewer's attention. The consequences part is the contrast that they need to be able to fully appreciate the anticipated pleasure (or relief from pain) they'll get as a result of your coaching.

72

LANDING PAGE

Common consequences could be:

- Lost opportunities
- Lack of sleep
- Financial strife
- Loss of relationships (lovers, kids, friends)
- Poor health
- Being alone
- Loss of significance
- Wasted potential
- Wasted time
- Substance abuse
- Emotional instability

These are all possible costs of not engaging in your coaching. Not everyone will experience all of these, but some may experience some of them. I'm not suggesting that you put a major focus on these because a little will go a long way here, but it's necessary to point out the *cost of inaction*.

COACHING LEADS FORMULA

**Exercise: What awful future pain(s) will your coaching prevent?**

_____

_____

_____

_____

_____

_____

_____

# Benefits

Now we get to focus on something we all like more—the positive.
We started off with the benefits in the headline, then referred to the
cost of inaction, and now we're going to dive back into the positive.
In coaching, we call that fractionation - the intention is to build trust
quickly. It's the same in marketing. You're intentionally taking your
potential clients from one side of the emotional spectrum to the
other. This lets them decide which side they want to land on.

As you learned earlier, there is an arc to a good hero's journey: life is
good, then it's not, and then it goes through a transformation where
life starts on the upswing again until there's a new normal that is
better than before. That's where we are now and NOW instead of
only talking about the biggest benefit, I want you to go into detail
about ALL the benefits that your coaching will provide your clients.

# LANDING PAGE

## Features versus benefits

A lot of coaches and folks starting out with marketing (and even old hands like myself) can mix up features and benefits. There is a time for both, so I want to explain the differences.

In a nutshell, benefits are what you're going to GET by using the features. In other words, a quick, clean, drilled hole is the benefit you get from a ¼" titanium drill bit with a chisel-cut edge. The features are ¼", titanium steel, chisel-cut, diamond-hardened edge.

When you're speaking to people and they haven't yet emotionally committed, generally you want to speak to the benefits. It's the solution they're seeking—the itch they need to scratch. They don't care how it gets scratched, just that it does. Once they emotionally commit to you and your solution, then the features come in to help justify their emotional decision. It's easy to get them confused, but they can be the difference between a page that converts visitors to clients and one that you just have to pay for and sits there not making a penny.

If you have a series of features (remember the difference—a hole or a drill bit), this is a key opportunity to showcase your features and the associated benefits of each one. Tell them things they'll get by working with you— what tangible effects they'll see in their lives. Will they feel more confident? Crush the next interview? Free up more time for loved ones? Lose weight and reduce medical bills?

When you're describing these features and benefits, try and put yourself in the role of a Hollywood writer. Set the scene: What do we see the client doing now? What are they saying? What are others saying about them? How are they acting now? What will they get to see or hear as a result of life after your coaching?

COACHING LEADS FORMULA

**Exercise:** What are the benefits working with you will produce for your clients? What value does your coaching deliver to them? Remember, be visual, specific, and use sensory words.

_____

_____

_____

_____

_____

_____

_____

_____

If your benefits fall under one idea or topic, then feel free to group them together under one title. That way you can organize the page in a logical manner and create a few buckets for your benefits. Think of areas of life and how your coaching benefits them, and how your client's life will be different in those areas (e.g.., financial, relationships, adventure, romance, spiritual, health, etc.).

## Authority

Authority is best delivered by demonstration. The power of showing someone through a story is unparalleled. With a good story, you can move mountains and influence the world. This part of the landing page is a tiny snippet of your full hero's journey, but it's critical to share.

You need to demonstrate two things here:

# LANDING PAGE

- First, that you've "been there, done that" and can understand what they're going through and can feel their pain.

- Second, that you have the knowledge and know the path to lead them forward so they don't fall victim to the same mistakes you did.

In this part of the landing page all you need is to demonstrate their biggest frustration or pain and identify with it.

Example: "I understand how debilitating inconsistent income can be—for years I couldn't plan more than a month in advance because I didn't know how much I'd be able to spend."

A little goes a long way here like in the Consequences section, but it builds a bond quickly. It says, "I'm one of you. I'm 'your people' because I've been there too."

You can also deliver authority through other people's words. Testimonials can be dual purpose here, serving as authority as well as social proof. Be careful to hand-pick the testimonials that specifically state how much their success was due to your coaching.

Another way to demonstrate authority is through statistics.

- How many years have you been working with clients?

- How many client transformations have you facilitated?

- How many hours have you saved clients?

- How much money have your clients made or saved because of your coaching?

- How many and which awards have you won?

- And so on…

These might not seem impressive to you, but I assure you—to your prospects, they'll be VERY impressive.

COACHING LEADS FORMULA

Numbers speak volumes to a select segment of the population. If your ideal client is one who works in numbers (engineers, finance, computer techs), then you will want to make sure to include numbers in your landing page. If you omit them, they will know you're NOT their people—because they talk in numbers rather than feeling language. It's always good to remember the different ways that people learn (visually, auditorily, emotionally, and through data). You've probably hit the first three already, but if you miss the last and your clients need it, your business will struggle.

# The Map

If you were transported to an unnamed location and had no idea where it was, but I said to you, "I will meet you in New York City under the clock at Grand Central Station in three weeks, and when I see you there I will give you $1 million," what would you think? You'd probably think, "that's great! That should be easy—let's go!"

But there are two problems: You don't know where you are, and you don't know where you're going in relation to where you are. In short, you need a map.

Your prospect who is on the landing page is in the same predicament. They need to be told or shown where to go and what will be waiting for them once they arrive.

If I had just told you to go to New York City without a reason or how to get there, you'd probably tell me no and laugh in my face. On the other hand, if I gave you a map to get there and a compelling reason to go, you would probably do your best to get to New York City, wouldn't you?

If your instructions are not explicit and easy to follow, your landing page visitors will simply abandon hope and click the "X" button. Poof! Your prospect is gone, never to return! Don't let them disappear because they're confused.

## LANDING PAGE

I remember when I had just started my former company. We had fifteen different types of bean seeds we sold. Some of our customers wanted more than a small packet of seeds, so we started to offer two additional sizes—a ½-lb. and a 1-lb. size for the homesteaders.

After we added the additional sizes we still kept on getting people who would order 16 one-ounce packets instead of a one-pound bag. I was curious, so I would call and ask, "Why didn't you order a one-pound bag instead of the 16 packets? It's one-fourth the cost!" Guess what the answer was? "I didn't know you had other sizes!"

We had made it difficult for the customer to find the additional size; we were confusing them. To see the other sizes, you had to click on a drop-down menu and select the size, but many people just saw the "BUY" button and clicked that instead.

You might be thinking, "yeah, but you made more money," and I'd argue that for every person who chose 16 one-ounce packets, we had ten people simply leave because they didn't see what they wanted.

The instructions must be clear and to the point. Give them the three steps they need to take in order to get their desired goal. If your goal is getting them on a call in order to qualify them for your coaching, then what steps do they have to take to get on that call?

**Step 1.** Click 'Apply' below

**Step 2.** Book your free coaching call

**Step 3.** Start living a stress-free life (or whatever their goal is)

If you have multiple steps that are required, group them under a category so it still looks simple and easy for the prospect to get their result. Keep it under four steps max, otherwise the prospects will think it's too complicated and probably go somewhere else.

## COACHING LEADS FORMULA

**Exercise:** What are the three big steps that your prospect needs to take in the next minute, day, or week that will get them on the road to fulfilling their dreams and annihilating their fears? Keep it to three if you can.

1. _____

2. _____

3. _____

Now you need to flesh out the details a bit. Talk about the benefits of each step—what your prospect will get out of each step and why they should bother to take that step. Remember the hole versus drill bit analogy. You want to describe the benefits, not the features. They care about what it will do for them, what they will have as a result, or who they will become.

**Exercise:** What benefits does each step provide your client?

1. _____

_____

_____

2. _____

_____

_____

3. _____

_____

_____

## LANDING PAGE

# Reinforcement

Now we get to use your Dream Client Identity work, transformation, and hero's journey work you did earlier. This is the part of the page where you will get to explain in more detail what your service can do for them. It's a way to build more rapport, and a side benefit is that you're going to be using lots of SEO (Search Engine Optimization)-rich keywords to describe things, so your landing page will rank high on the search engines.

Just like your conversation hook, you want to show your prospects you understand their BIG problem. Start off by identifying with your prospect: "I understand how you feel..."

Then emphasize their dreams and what would make their lives easier and better in the short-term as well. By doing this, you're taking them from pleasure, to pain, back to pleasure—it'll help to appease the analytical side of their brains if they're not yet convinced.

After you describe their dreams, you want to step up with your authority and credibility, describing how you've been there (or helped hundreds of others just like them). Then give them the rough outline of how the process will unfold and the steps you will use to take them through it. These details will appease the data-driven crowd.

Finally, urge them on with a call to action. What is the first step they need to take to start on this journey of transformation and discovery?

The first time you write this, it will be long. I recommend no more than two paragraphs. Just like with your conversation hook, you want it to sound natural, so I suggest you practice speaking it out loud until it sounds good to you. Keep improving it until you can't simplify it anymore and still convey what you need to say.

# Video

We all love to watch videos! It's the most consumed media on the internet, so much so that YouTube gets 500 HOURS uploaded to their platform every single minute. YouTube is also the second- ranked search engine behind Google itself. People love to watch videos.

Twenty years ago when I was getting started in graphic design, I used to refer to Photoshop as instant gratification because you could edit photos instantly, swap backgrounds, change the colors, or add text easily. But then I discovered video editing. WOW! You could stitch different clips together, you could edit the sound, add music, even motion graphics. I described it as instant orgasm because it was such a richer and more robust medium than just single images. It was thirty images per second WITH SOUND!

Video is more than that though; it's a representation of you—your voice, your mannerisms, your vocal inflections, your facial expressions. Short of being there in person with your client, video is the second-best thing. Some might even argue it's better because when someone views your video, they can do so in the comfort of their home, where they can consume your video without worrying about being judged. That gives you the opportunity to build a powerful rapport in a short amount of time.

The video is your chance to share your big why—why you believe your coaching can help them. It's essentially everything we've already worked on up until now, but in video form.

There will be some people (a lot, probably) who jump directly to the video, so it's important to include one in your page.

## Video Gear

Fear not, dear reader. Even though I want you to give video a try, you don't have to worry about having amazing production values. You don't need to go out and buy thousands of dollars in equipment or pay a high-end editor to create your masterpiece. You probably already have a perfectly adequate camera that will create video that is higher quality than most video recorders were ten (even five) years ago...that's right, your cell phone. Many of today's cell phones can record at a minimum HD video, and some are capable of 8K video, which is WAY more than you need!

If you just hold your phone in front of you and speak to the camera, with good lighting and minimal background sound, your videos will be exactly what you need. In fact, many handheld, impromptu videos perform better than slick, high-budget productions because your audience can feel the authenticity. A word on sound though: If you can, having a separate microphone that is positioned close to your mouth (on your label or ball cap) will improve the video quality enormously. Bad sound can ruin an otherwise amazing video. See the resources section for suggestions on equipment.

Don't fret though—it doesn't have to be complex. It could be just you talking into your cell phone, the webcam, or a digital camera, if you have one. Or if you really are afraid of the camera, you can do a voice-over (meaning just you talking into the microphone) and can use video that looks like it relates to what you're talking about. Keep the video short—three-to-five minutes. That might not sound like long, but you'd be surprised how much you can say within five short minutes!

Remember to pique the viewer's interest by posing a question first, just like you did with your Conversation Hook. Ideally it should be the big problem your client came to your landing page searching for the solution. Next, present your solution to the problem (meaning your coaching plan).

There's an old format for selling that is very appropriate for a short video: Problem, Solution, Offer. You want to state the problem, talk about your solution, and close with an offer/call to action.

## Putting It All Together

According to Hick's law, the more choices a person has, the longer they will take to make a decision. That's why there's only seven elements here on the landing page. A landing page is meant to direct them to one specific action—ideally getting on a call with you. So keep it simple and direct.

I'd also recommend against having a navigation bar at the top because it distracts from the intention and could have the visitor leaving the landing page without consuming the content you worked so hard to create!

There's lots of stuff that needs to also be included in a full website, like a contact page, a privacy page, refunds, guarantee, etc., but I recommend putting those links in the footer where the visitor can find it if they must, but the average person won't get distracted by it. But those elements aren't necessary to create if all you're doing is a stand-alone landing page, which is all I think you need to start off, and what I'm suggesting you put together first.

Once you have all these elements, put them onto paper or into a single document (PowerPoint or Google Slides are easy to use for very simple graphic design ideas). After you get the text and the order right, you can hand this off to a designer, who will make it look amazing.

## LEAD MAGNET

If anything in this chapter felt like it was overwhelming and you need help, feel free to reach out to me and my team to see how we might be able to make your life a little easier!  Go to https://getcfl.com/book - I want you out there changing the world one client at a time, and if I can help you get there, I'd be honored!

# COACHING LEADS FORMULA

# 11. Lead Magnet

The assets I referred to earlier are things you create once and then allow them to do their work. Just like building a house and then leasing it to tenants, this asset will pay for itself for years— just put the work into creating it, be patient and allow it to work its magic.

In the marketing world, we call one of these assets a lead magnet. A lead magnet is designed to accomplish a very specific purpose and that is acquiring a lead! Technically it's taking a visitor and putting their contact information in your database for future follow up.

A lead magnet can be just about anything of value. Whatever can help solve a small (first step) chunk of the problem your client is experiencing. A lead magnet could be:

- a book (like this)
- a report or whitepaper (but don't have that be the title!)
- a quiz (very popular at the moment)
- a cheat sheet
- a top-ten list
- a mistakes to avoid list
- a mini-course (they pique people's competitive and self-discovery nature)
- a template (something they will want to use often)

## COACHING LEADS FORMULA

- a video (could be a training or webinar)

- an audio recording (a podcast or guided meditation)

- a checklist (something that will help them daily)

- an article or interview of an industry leader

Even though I know you will find your most responsive communication method, I want to encourage you to try to master video presentations. For most people, video is the best way to connect and reach them. Video provides an amazing opportunity to explain your service as well as build powerful rapport with your prospects.

Video can also be easily repurposed into many other mediums. You can repost to various social channels, you can use the audio for a podcast, and the transcript for blogs.

Finally, people LOVE videos! It's like TV but easier, which is borne out by the fact that videos can increase purchase activity by 80%! Because of this, the big web services like Google, YouTube, Facebook, Twitter, and LinkedIn all favor video and will love you more if you have video on your website.

Now that you know the benefits of using video, I know you're going to give it a shot! If you are scared or worried, don't be. Have faith in yourself and know you're going to improve. The first time you wrote in cursive, I'm sure you couldn't even read it, but eventually through practice you got better, right? Producing your video will be the same way and the more you practice, the happier you will be with your video result. Of course, once you have created your video, I have four tips that will help your video perform better.

There are a few schools of thought on assets and whether to charge for them.

# LEAD MAGNET

If they're free, they're often called a lead magnet, meaning you're attracting (like a magnet) leads into your sphere of influence. If you're offering it for money (often a small amount), it's referred to as a tripwire product because, when they buy this small product, you'll offer a larger product that offers to solve a bigger problem or provides more value.

The benefit of offering a free lead magnet is that the bar is lower and your conversions into leads will be higher. Most people carefully guard the privacy of their email, so it truly is a demonstration of trust on their part to share their email with you. When they give you their email, it is the first step of many along the road of their commitment to you, hopefully ending in them becoming a client.

Both routes work well, but whichever you choose to take, I suggest you must deliver true and undeniable value.

So, if that email is so valuable, how do you get someone to part with it? By doing what I spoke of already: delivering value. By showing them something new that can help them, you build authority, likeability, trust, and reciprocity. These are four powerful psychological motivators.

On your landing page you will have a testimonial section. That demonstrates social proof, which is yet another powerful psychological motivator. If you have limited spots available in your coaching programs, you've hit on nearly all the motivators by also including scarcity!

## Giving away the farm

Some coaches I speak to are worried about giving too much information. They feel that if they give it away, no one will buy a product or service from them if they can get it for free. There are two simple answers.

First, there's always more to discover. If you're learning and growing, you're going to continue to have more and more to offer your clients. It's inevitable that you're going to get more skilled, have more knowledge, be more efficient, know more people, etc. So don't let that worry you.

Second, even though you're pouring your heart out with this information, you are only showing them a piece of the puzzle. They don't know what they don't know.

What you are giving them is only a small tidbit of the entire journey of transformation you have in store for them. In fact, if you showed them the whole journey, many of your prospects wouldn't want it because they wouldn't believe it's possible yet. You have to meet them where they are NOW, which will change once they get a taste of what's possible. Remember when you were on this journey. Did you think where you are at NOW was possible? I'm guessing you might have wanted it to be possible, but didn't yet believe it. If you did, that's AMAZING! Your clients will get incredible results and quickly because your beliefs were/are so powerful!

When you are building and creating your first asset, or your lead magnet (in video format hopefully,) you want to include:

1. **Catchy Title** - You need to have a title that is interesting and makes them want to know more. Numbers are great: "Top 5 Ways to Relax at Any Moment" or "Drop 6 Pounds in 6 Weeks." People will understand that. You also want to speak to their pain point and how you're going to solve it.

# LEAD MAGNET

2. **Obvious Expert** - You want it to position you as the obvious expert. It's another step on the road to trusting you—you can do this many ways, but often it's in the stories you've told, any testimonials you've included, and the bio section. In each of these, you want to remember: Make it about the client, not yourself.

3. **Key Problem** - What is the big problem they're trying to solve? I call it the key problem because it unlocks the door for you to build more trust, authority, and offer additional products/services. Keep in mind, this is the problem THEY think they have, not the REAL problem you know they have. Use their language when voicing this problem.

4. **Big Solution** - What is your solution that is quick and easy for them to implement and get results within a specific time frame? This isn't the big, overall problem; this is a small, baby-step problem you can help them overcome. Give them the 50,000- foot view in this video. Speak of the transformation rather than the specifics of the tools/techniques. Talk about their dreams here, not details!

6. **Teaching** - If it's a PDF or video, walk them through three-to-five steps of the process to fix this primary problem. This is the opportunity for you to shine and teach. This is the #1 piece of the puzzle—the problem they THINK they have right now, not the larger, actual problem. If it's a checklist or something short like that, make it exceptionally valuable. For instance, how could it save them time by shortcutting something for them?

    The teaching has to include a win for the client. They want to know they've achieved something from your coaching that they couldn't have done alone or in as short a time.

7. **Call to Action** - This is where you invite them to continue on the journey with you. If they found this useful and valuable, ask them to book a call and see how they can keep the momentum going.

## COACHING LEADS FORMULA

Your lead magnet has the potential to inspire them to action. Your goal is to get them to book a call with you so you can get more detail about their challenges. In that call you'll be able to really dig in to what is bothering them and understand if you can truly help them. The beauty of this lead magnet, which is meant to be consumed by the client in 10-15 minutes, is that once you outline it, you can produce it in an afternoon and it can rapidly start getting those leads lining up and knocking on your door! This is how you maximize your time and how you get a consistent stream of leads who turn into clients.

Lead magnets are an incredibly powerful way to get your leads lining up at your door, begging for your business. You're essentially cloning yourself here—multiplying yourself in a way that lets you have the greatest impact you possibly can. It will also pre-qualify many of those people who might be tempted to get on the phone with you so that only the most anxious and excited people actually make that call to you.

These are some common mistakes you'll want to avoid:

- **Having too many steps:** Layout the path and focus the lead magnet ONLY on step one. What's the first thing they need to do? Don't go overboard and teach too much or you may overwhelm them.

- **Using too much text:** If it's a PDF, keep the fonts large, use lots of bullets, photos, and callouts, and keep it under four pages of content. Again, you want it visually appealing, but also very simple. It needs to be easy to implement to get them a quick win.

- **Having a boring title:** Keep your title interesting, to the point, and address the problem and the dream client. Don't be vague or you will confuse and lose.

## LEAD MAGNET

- **Focusing on the wrong subject:** Occasionally you won't have much response from the lead magnet. That usually means you're not addressing a real problem—you're addressing a superficial problem. The key to the game is testing and practice. If things aren't working, adjust and retest. When a baby is learning to walk, it takes falling down a few times before it can stand up and walk. Same for you - you're learning to walk, so you might fall down a few times, but just keep getting up and you'll be running in no time!!

If you'd like help writing your email sequence, getting your lead magnet set up or your landing pages designed, visit us at https://getcfl.com and set up a call so we can discuss your needs.

94

GET THE WORD OUT

# 12. Get the Word Out

## Next Steps

Well, NOW WHAT? You've made an amazing, beautiful, magnificent baby, so now what do you do with it? The first step is to show it off wherever you have the biggest following! For many people that'll be their website, but it could also be their social media or their existing email list. Put it on your bios and About pages for all your social media locations.

You need to promote it everywhere you think your dream client might be and/or may see it. This is like going fishing: the more hooks in the water, the more chance you're going to land a big fish!

We talked about this in Chapter 6. Go back and review the exercises to refresh your ideas about your dream client and where they might hang out. What forums do they frequent or websites do they follow? You'll want to become part of those communities and offer to help. Eventually people will become interested in who you are and look you up. Then guess what? You've got the link right in your bio already!

So how can you do that and not spend forever making posts and different videos?

Simply, you take your lead magnet and repurpose it. Change it slightly, make it appropriate for the platform, and poof—you've got a dozen different ways to share the same piece of information!

95

COACHING LEADS FORMULA

If you've already made a video, then this will be a breeze.. Because you won't have to make a video for anything else. You can just just edit the video you already have.

# Where and How

Here are some ideas of how you can repurpose just about anything, including video. Obviously technology is quickly evolving, so this list is going to change and evolve with time.

- **Blog Post** - You can write a page or a blog post on your website about the topic. If you did a video, you could have a transcription made of the video, and then edit it into a cohesive article.

- **LinkedIn Article** - That same blog post can become an article on LinkedIn that you can promote to your network. Very useful for establishing your authority even before you speak to a prospect.

- **Email** - If you have a list, you can create a valuable email that teaches what you showed in the lead magnet. You might also break it up into a mini email-delivered course (most people hate long emails).

- **Facebook** - This is obvious, but bears repeating. Post the article in a super concise format to your Facebook page, story, or reels. Try not to send them off Facebook - they like to keep its members on the site and will not promote your post much if you send them to an external link. Instead, let your link from the bio direct them to your website.

- **Instagram** - You could cut a clip from the video and use it as a post, story, or reel. You could also use a quote from your video or PDF with a nice picture in the background.

- **Reddit** - Just as with Facebook groups, you will want to provide value, answer questions—give more than you get, essentially. But once you've invested enough in the community, you'll be able to post your link so it can add value to the forum.

## GET THE WORD OUT

Each platform will have its own unique requirements. Remember that they are designed for different audiences. You may need to adapt the posting to the specific platform in addition to the specific person that you want to read the post.

The most important thing is to remain consistent. There are a lot of ways out there to automate posting, which helps to batch content so you only have to hammer this stuff out one or two nights a month. If you don't know how to do something, look on various freelancer sites to find people who can help for a very reasonable fee. All you need to do is get them the video, audio, or finished PDF and they can create ten different formats for you to post.

# COACHING LEADS FORMULA

THANK YOU PAGE

# 13. Thank You Page

After folks have signed up for your lead magnet and clicked the "Submit" button, the next page they should see should be the "Thank You" page. This is your opportunity to really emphasize the value you're going to be providing them with your lead magnet.

You want to create another video where you will provide some extra teaching on the elements of the lead magnet - especially if it's a written document like a pdf or an eBook. Perhaps it's a deeper understanding, or perhaps it's the next step in the process. Whatever it is, you want to really build value and authority.

**Rephrase each of these suggestions with your own voice and style, but here's the idea of how the video should flow:**

**You:** "Thank you, check your email in the next few minutes for [LEAD MAGNET NAME]. I love helping people with [BIG PROBLEM]— and if it's okay with you I'd like to give you something on top of the [LEAD MAGNET NAME], which I'll get back to in a moment."

*You've thanked them and pre-framed the lead magnet on top of teasing a free gift, which will get them to watch the video a bit longer.*

## COACHING LEADS FORMULA

**You:** "Because you downloaded [LEAD MAGNET NAME] I'm guessing you want to know how to overcome [BIG PROBLEM]. I know some folks are impatient, so I thought I'd do a quick video explaining the [THREE] steps I talk about in [LEAD MAGNET NAME].

*You're confirming their problem and promising to give additional content all while confirming you know their struggles.*

**You:** "The first/second/third step to solve [BIG PROBLEM] is…

*Teach each step, but keep the pretty big picture—the 50,000-foot view—you want the steps to be no more than 2-3 minutes each.*

**You:** "Wow, that was a lot of content, I know! But I'd like to give you a heads up that if you'd like to hop on a call with me, we can go over this stuff in much more detail. There should be a button down below where you can book a call with me."

*You're reminding them to book a call if they want to get specific with their needs and how you can help THEM specifically.*

You: "Thank you for watching to the end! I hope you found it as useful as I did when I was first learning it. If you're still watching, then maybe you haven't clicked the button below yet. I love working with [DREAM CLIENT IDENTITY] and would love to talk more about your [BIG PROBLEM]. It will be a coaching call, not a sales call. If I feel like I can help you more, I will let you know at the end of the call. If I don't honestly think you're a fit for my coaching, I can refer you to resources I DO think will help if you would like. Either way, I hope you enjoyed this video and I look forward to connecting with you one day!"

*You want to let them know you're going to continue to add and provide value for them, helping them to solve their challenges. You also want to guide them to that call because on the call you're going to get a chance to learn more specifically how and if you can help them.*

## THANK YOU PAGE

Other elements to include on your Thank You page:

- Testimonials, either in picture and text format or some short videos. It always helps to add additional social proof.

- Links to your social media.

- Additional, relevant, free guides they might be interested in (if you have those).

- Popular content (if you have a blog or other articles on the website).

# COACHING LEADS FORMULA

# 14. Magic of Email

You have created your Dream Client Identity, and know their pains, their desires, their frustrations, and what they long for more than anything else.

You've learned how to create rapport by sharing your transformation through the power of storytelling.

You've created an outstanding landing page that entices prospects to give you their email address.

So now what?

I'd like to first congratulate you because you've crossed a tremendous hurdle by getting your website finished! Of course, the point of the website is to create customers (a.k.a. clients). But second only to the website is the value of email!

You might be thinking, "Email is dead." Let me tell you—email isn't dead!

Think about how valuable email is. 99% of people will check their email daily and often multiple times a day! It's also a dedicated way you can communicate with your people. If Facebook or Twitter decided to ban you or shut down your account for some reason, what would you do?

It wouldn't matter as long as you have an email list, because you would still be able to communicate with your clients! Email is the most reliable and quickest way to get in touch with your clients aside from text messaging.

Numbers vary, but for a super-responsive email list, your list could be worth up to $10 per email sent (per month) or as little as $0.50 per email/per month. If you have 2,500 people on your email list, that could easily be worth thousands of dollars per month!

Email's where it's at. It's what you need to have in place to set yourself up to having a consistent income, which I know you want!

There are three different types of email you can send. Each type is used for a specific purpose:

- Broadcast Emails
- Sales Sequence
- Nurture Sequence

First let's tackle the type you're probably not going to use very often:

## Broadcast Emails

Those of you who are old enough to remember when TV came from an antenna instead of a cable might recall what the network names ABC or NBC stand for. They stand for the "American Broadcasting Company and the National Broadcasting Company," respectively. The concept of broadcasting has been around for years. The first time the word was used was to describe radio long before tv or the internet was invented.

Broadcast means to spread or scatter and that's what you're going to be doing. When you send a broadcast email, you send it out far and wide and as a one-time message. It's usually a manually sent email that you've prepared for a reason. You may have seen or received the "Oops, made a mistake" email from someone or a newsletter that is an updated version every time it is delivered.

MAGIC OF EMAIL

The big difference between broadcast emails and sequenced ones is that broadcast emails are usually sent to announce something. For instance, perhaps you got mentioned in an article or even just wrote an amazing new blog post. A broadcast email would be a great way to promote that. It is also used for time-sensitive events such as sales or discounts.

# Why Sequence It?

Remember the dating analogy and how it takes getting to know them a bit, building rapport, and establishing trust first before taking them home to meet mom?

That relationship-building is what a sequence can do. You have the opportunity to send a predetermined number of emails that allow you to duplicate yourself, remain consistently in front of your prospects, and will create that consistent income that separates successful businesses from those who fail.

The magic of sequences is that you do it once and then forget it. You do not have to remember to reach out to people. You can avoid the headache of having to come up with new and interesting content all the time. You don't get discouraged because it's the fifth time you've heard the word *no*. The magic is in the automated repetition of it by creating those next dates and allowing your lead to get to know you—all in the background without you having to lift a finger!

Why are sequences so valuable? Because you will be able to:

1. **Stay Top of Mind** - Incredibly important! Your lead might not be ready for your coaching today, but if they don't forget about you, when they finally ARE ready you want them to think of you.

2. **Deliver Value** - Again, this is about building rapport, establishing authority, and creating trust. You can do that through educational emails that are enjoyable to read and deliver content that impresses them.

# COACHING LEADS FORMULA

3. **Prompt a Conversation** - You will occasionally want to ask them questions. It creates a true conversation where you ask for information. It also says, "I need you," and engages them. When they've answered a question and helped you, they will enjoy being part of the solution and are more likely to commit to your coaching.

4. **Prompt Action** - In addition to asking questions, you can have calls to action in the body of the email or more subtly in your email postscript or even in your email signature. This allows them to make the move when they're ready rather than submit to a high-stress sales call. This is how you avoid the slimy sales feeling.

A formula like this is how you will be able to consistently convert leads into paying customers without you having to go knocking on doors or cold calling people all the time. By automating yourself, you will be able to have the impact you want and the life you deserve.

Best Practices in Email:

- **Subject Line:** An interesting subject line that invites curiosity will make or break your open rates. Take note of fun ones you get from others and use something similar in yours!

- **Pattern Interrupt:** You want to use a pattern interrupt to get them focused on your email. You can do it with a question, a story, a visual—however you do it, it gets them invested in YOUR email through curiosity.

- **Storytelling:** Stories are the way you can communicate without telling. Stories and metaphors are an excellent way to deliver information to the subconscious without being annoying. They are also the key to getting people to open each and every email because you're entertaining while educating!

## MAGIC OF EMAIL

- **Open Loops:** An open loop is a cliffhanger. It's the secret weapon that virtually guarantees your emails will be opened. The brain desperately wants completion and it will seek it out by just about any means available. If you leave a story unfinished and say, "To be continued…," you will induce an itch in the reader's subconscious that they will want to scratch by reading the next email and finishing the story!

- **Deliver Value:** By sharing value, you're investing in the rapport bank account of give, give, give, then ask. Don't ask before investing or they will question why they should commit. Make it obvious why your coaching will be worth it.

- **Postscript:** A PS will give you the ability to put in a subtle call to action or an unexpected twist or fact. It's a way to engage without being overt.

- **Encourage Response:** When you ask questions, you create engagement. Ask a direct, big, burning question. Keep it minimal and effective but ask them to reply. Assure them that you will read every response. By doing this, you will be able to get some incredibly valuable information from your list.

- **Talk Normally:** Keep things easy and simple to understand. Keep the sentences short and make it conversational, like you're talking with a friend or close associate.

- **Use Formatting:** Using bolding, bullets, italics. Those are all ways to visually break up your email so it reads easier.

- **Limit CTAs:** You want each email you send to have one theme and intention. Keep that in mind as you write it. By keeping it focused and simple, you will ensure that you move the lead to a client. Don't muddy the waters by having more than one subject or call to action. Remember, "If you confuse, you will lose."

COACHING LEADS FORMULA

- **Stay Relevant:** Segmentation is a way to communicate with a prospect on topics that interest them. You don't want to send them emails about things they have no interest in. That is the beauty of segmentation. If you have an email talking about anxiety, you don't want to then send them an email about keto. You want to help them learn about anxiety! By tracking what links they click on, you will remain relevant and interesting to them and keep your email open rates super high!

## Sales Sequences

When you have a product that you'd like someone to buy or a program you want them to sign up for, a sales sequence is a way to get them warmed up to buy.

It's also a way to be more relevant and deliver information they want to know about. Let's say a lead/prospect is signed up for your general nurture campaign and they click on a link you had included about a course on anxiety. In effect, they have raised their hand and said, "I want to learn more about anxiety!" At that point you will pause the general nurture sequence and start a conversation with them all about anxiety and how you can help with that challenge.

The details of how this all works isn't important right now. There are services out there that make it very easy to implement, and if you need to you can always hire someone to help you with the functionality. The important part is keeping things relevant for them, and now you know what's possible!

Through a series of emails, you educate the lead on the topic, which establishes your authority and reinforces that you can help them with that challenge. Then, because you have established trust and authority, you can make them an offer designed to help them with that challenge.

108

# MAGIC OF EMAIL

A sales sequence is a specific outcome-oriented series of emails. Once they've run their course and if they don't generate a sale, the lead will go back onto your general nurture campaign. This allows you to constantly remain relevant and top of mind with your lead.

A sales sequence is what will follow the lead magnet submission. This email sequence is what you'll set up to be sent after they hit the download button on your landing page. It is designed to be sent over a series of days (which can vary in number), but this is the basic idea below.

Keep in mind you're not sending every day—the day number represents the days **after they hit the submit button** on your landing page.

1. *Day 0* - The first email will be the delivery of the lead magnet. They won't have access to the lead magnet until they verify they have a real email. So you want to first deliver the PDF or the link to the training.

2. *Day 1* - Today you will want to welcome them! Say hello and introduce yourself. Let them get to know you and your personal story a bit. You can use some of your hero's story, but simplify and edit it a little here.

3. *Day 2* - You'll want to speak to the value of the transformation the lead magnet can provide. This is because not everyone has downloaded it yet or even consumed it. Offer a testimonial or a story about how powerful it can be. Use some of your information from the Benefits section.

4. *Day 4* - Educate by explaining how they can get the most out of the lead magnet. Can you address common objections or even difficulties people have had in implementing what they learned from the lead magnet? Yes. This is also an opportunity to preframe any objections you might get with the coaching (time, money, etc.).

# COACHING LEADS FORMULA

5. *Day 6* - Answer questions. By now you know the common questions you get in response to the lead magnet. You want to provide further value by giving the answers to those questions.

6. *Day 8* - Keep educating and foreshadow the offer. By this time you have built some value, but here you really want to add substantively to that investment account. Continue educating them on the transformation (less about the "how" and more about the "why"). This is to get them to buy into the belief it's possible. In your PS or as your last point, foreshadow that the next email will be a call to action—an offer.

7. *Day 9* - Sales time. In this email, you will ask for the offer—don't try and sell; just make the offer. You can list out some key benefits, but more than that, you want them thinking, "Now is the time," rather than "What else do I get?" If there is a time-constraint or a real sense of scarcity ("only X number of clients"), this email is the place to announce it. You can mention any bonuses you may include and if there is a limitation (first X clients, next XX hours, etc.).

8. *Day 10* - Sales reminder. Remind them of your offer, give a recap, and then tell them whether anything will not be available after X hours.

Wow, that's it - I know it seems like a lot, but in reality it's only 8 emails. Although it's not set in stone, it's a good outline to use for your sales sequence. The process will naturally be different for everyone, but this is a good place to start.

# MAGIC OF EMAIL

If there is no sale, the lead then gets added back into the nurture sequence where they will continue to be reminded of your coaching, continue to get value, and continue to build that relationship with you. The net effect will be that once their problem becomes big enough and they start to seek out assistance, you will be the first one to come to mind. This brings us to the next type of sequence—the nurture sequence.

## Nurture Sequence

I have been told by many different teachers and coaches that whenever you are trying to teach a new topic to someone, you want to educate, inspire, and entertain. By doing all three you will prime the mind to take in new information and open up what is possible in their understanding.

When I hear the word entertain, the image of a comedian on stage with a microphone in hand comes to mind. But that's not the only way to entertain. In an email, the best way to entertain is with the use of storytelling. You've already experienced its impact when you were writing your own story of transformation. Now you get to apply that formula within your nurture sequence.

The primary purpose of the nurture sequence is to remain top of mind with your leads. The second and just as important is to deliver value and position you as the obvious choice when they finally feel they've reached the point they need to hire a coach.

Most people who write emails do so in a very boring style and that's why you don't read so many of the ones you receive. Occasionally there are those who send emails that are written like correspondence from a penpal. They invite you into their lives and weave events and knowledge in and out of the stories so much that you look forward to reading the next email.

The way you can achieve that kind of following is by doing a few specific things.

## COACHING LEADS FORMULA

The first thing to do is to use open loops in your writing. Open loops are when you break a story in the middle just after the climax and hold the resolution back until the next email. It's the same way that a cliffhanger in your favorite dramatic series on TV works. The season-ending cliffhanger has you talking about it and wishing the next season would hurry up and get here. The psychological trigger is that the brain wants completion. Something that is not completed makes your brain uncomfortable.

You can break up a story over several emails as well if it's a particularly long story that has multiple moments of drama. Open and close the email with the storytelling and have the meat in the middle be the teaching segment.

The best way to write these is to do so in a long text document so that you can see how the stories connect to one another and identify the moments of climax in each story where you would interrupt and close the email. Another way to do it is to write each story separately from beginning to end and then decide where you can use the climactic moments in each one to break them up and close an email. You can always break it by saying, "I'll get back to XYZ in a little bit, but first I want to talk about...," or something to that extent.

You can also utilize a fun signature line that is related to the story too. I have a story I tell about our very sweet pig, named "Miss Pigg," and in the sign off, instead of simply writing, "Theo Bill," I'll write, "Theo 'Pig Sitter' Bill" to make it funny. Or another story I talk about is with someone who convinced me to get my degree. I signed off that email with "Theo 'finally graduated' Bill."

# MAGIC OF EMAIL

**Exercise:** What are the three stories you could tell with the moral lesson you can teach about? And what are the unique sign-offs you can use for them?

1. _____

   _____

   _____

2. _____

   _____

   _____

3. _____

   _____

   _____

One of the biggest hurdles new writers have is they think they don't have a story to tell. They are wrong. Stories are everywhere. Pay attention to your day, your week, and life. There is a constant flow of stories with moral lessons to be found in the most mundane of circumstances. Use them. Choose some activity or event with your kids or coworkers or a client and imagine a story you can craft. Just remember the Before-During-After framework you learned earlier and you'll be fine.

## COACHING LEADS FORMULA

When you're trying to create the story, a good place to start is with what you want the takeaway to be. Once you know that, you can frame just about any event into it as a teaching moment. For example, the other day I was composing a story and it kept going on and on until I realized I didn't have an outcome for the audience in mind. The minute I decided on the outcome, the story fell into place easily.

Another thing folks struggle with is how long to run the nurture sequence. Obviously except for your first time writing the sequence, it's free so I'd suggest it be as long as you can make it, maybe even up to a year. If you send an email every week, that's only 52 emails; however, so you don't get too overwhelmed, shoot for 16 emails initially. That works out to four months of staying top of mind with an email every week, or six months if you send one every ten days instead.

Now you ask, "What do I include in the emails?" If you don't have 16 individual topics (the meat in the middle) to talk about, you could split things into a series. With only 16 emails, I am sure that you could come up with four topics that have four steps each.

Now, add in those six or eight stories at the beginning and end of the emails, and you've got a powerful nurture sequence!

---

**Exercise:** What are the four topics you could teach about and how can you break them up into four different steps or different emails?

1. _____

_____

_____

_____

# MAGIC OF EMAIL

2. _____

_____

_____

_____

3. _____

_____

_____

_____

4. _____

_____

_____

_____

When telling stories, the key is to be brief, keep your words simple, and your sentences and lines short. Try and keep your emails to a reading level of about the fourth grade. I know it might not make the most sense when you want to build authority, but believe me—it is better. Here's why: If the prospect is busy and in scan mode, they'll skip over the big words and miss the point. Most of us scan the email to see if it's worth reading. That's why the subject line and opening is important.

## COACHING LEADS FORMULA

Just for fun, I tested the paragraph above and it came out to grade 5.2 - so you can see how difficult it is to keep it simple! If you want to give it a try, you can use the readability checker here: https://www.webfx.com/tools/read-able/

Your lead has enough on their plate with a busy work, life, and the challenges they're facing. You don't want to add to their difficulty by forcing their brain to consume additional calories deciphering some postgraduate-level verbiage.

Keep it simple. When you confuse, you lose.

The last thing to remember is to include a call to action email every four emails or so. You could have a testimonial, a case study, or a story about a particular client and the benefits they received. Offer your prospect a CTA that asks them to book a call with you and you're set up!

Okay, I lied. I admit it. I said I wanted you to create 16 emails—now you have 20, with the fifth in the sequence being a sales/CTA one. You now have five months' worth of content!

I cannot stress enough that this sequencing concept is the make-or-break tool for your success. It can make your business one that is prosperous or one that is so much work and has such inconsistent income that you either quit being a coach or only do it part-time.

I want you to be a successful and THRIVING coach! Not only so you can fulfill your dreams, but also so all those folks out there who need your services will benefit. Getting these straightforward systems implemented and running on autopilot is where it starts.

## Email and technology

There are many email providers out there that can give you the tools you need to build your sequences.

Don't get discouraged because there's so many out there. You can spend as much or as little as you want when shopping for email service providers. The bare minimum you will need is simply the ability to send an automated sequence once your lead enters their email into a form.

Then the system automatically will send the lead magnet and follow-up emails.

Depending on your budget, you can use something as simple as MailChimp or as complicated as InfusionSoft (I don't recommend starting with that though).

Each software will have its own tutorials, and some will even have great templates of sequences already set up so you can simply overwrite the text.

Don't get discouraged or overwhelmed—there's lots of help and resources out there!

# COACHING LEADS FORMULA

# 15. Your Offer

Over the past 5 years of being in the coaching world, I have encountered some amazing people, but many of them don't make a full-time living from their coaching. Either through a fear of money, inability to ask their worth, or not understanding the skills to market, sell and close, the average coach makes far less than $25,0000 a year. If you do a quick LinkedIn search you'll find over one million coaches - and according to MarketData website, in 2022 coaching is supposed to be a $1.34 billion industry. When you do the math, that's about $500 each!

If you are not making enough money to even support yourself, how are you going to expand your business, impact more people, and change more lives? The answer is, of course, you can't do that when you're trying to make ends meet. Working multiple jobs, being burned out, undercharging your value, or having to take free clients because you need the referral will not make you successful!

I know coaching feels good. Trust me—I'm a coach as well, and I LOVE it. Seeing the light of a new reality dawn on a client for the first time or the bright supernova of a massive breakthrough is something you can't put a price tag on!

## COACHING LEADS FORMULA

Without sufficient income, though, so many everyday things—putting food on the table, a roof over your head, clothes on your back or even just having time off to recharge and recuperate so that you can handle the challenges of YOUR life—become very difficult. Add to that not being able to have the time, energy, and space to continue growing, learning, or working on your business so it can grow and you will SOON feel like you are in a swamp up to your waist in alligators.

There is a saying that was coined in the '50s by Cyril Parkinson. It goes like this: "The time it takes to complete a task will expand to the time that is given to it." According to Parkinson's Law, if you give someone ten minutes or ten hours, it will take a person that much time to accomplish the task.

I also think that a person will live up to the expectations someone makes of them. So I am here asking you to step up and become the coach I'm certain you are capable of! You can be one who is making full-time (and much better) income and changing thousands of lives in the process!

Money is simply a concept. It is and has been represented by many things. American Indians used shells, the Greeks used gold and silver, and Americans now use the dollar bill, which is nothing more than a piece of paper that is worth whatever we say it is worth and allows us to exchange things of value between people. I would argue that your coaching has value. In fact, probably life-changing value!

We can be a slave to money, but again it's simply a concept. If we change what it MEANS, we take control of the concept. When you think about charging value for your services, think of the value in relation to your clients' lives and the success or goals that they will achieve tomorrow because of your coaching today. In fact, by charging your true value, you're actually demanding them to grow to meet that expectation.

# YOUR OFFER

Who will your client become because of your service and product?

If you charge less, aren't you saying they are worth less and, in effect, lowering the expectation of what they can be and accomplish?

Don't be the mirror to their mediocrity; be the guide to their greatness.

The more you charge, the more confident you are in your ability to achieve that outcome (assuming they do the work) and the better the outcome will be. It is as simple as that. Your client is responsible for the value they receive, but you have to create the expectation (and deliver) that they will achieve that value.

Last year I took my mother out for a birthday dinner at an expensive restaurant. We had eaten there the previous two years on her birthday and were always impressed by the service, food, and atmosphere. This year though, our experience was different. We didn't get the special extras that we had the years before.

The quality of the food, the atmosphere, and the service were the same, but because we had one outcome in mind and reality was disagreeing with that expectation, we thought we didn't get the same value. It was up to ME to determine if I had received value. The food was still delicious. The service was excellent and the space hadn't changed. It was entirely up to me to decide the value I assigned.

The same goes for your clients. Give them the expectation that you will be the force that assures that they achieve their outcome and they'll be blown away. You will have created a reality that creates value, which you can charge well for.

Obviously, one size doesn't fit everyone as far as how much to charge, what to include in a package, etc. If it were that easy, life would be pretty boring, right? When it comes to coaching, there are a multitude of different pricing options. I don't want to suggest which method or option is the best fit for you or your clients, but I can give you some guidelines and examples to consider.

COACHING LEADS FORMULA

I've arranged these examples in order of value and income (per transaction) as well as the number of potential clients. Keep in mind that as the price goes up, the amount of rapport you need to build goes up along with the income potential.

## Membership Model
*Income: $ (low) Reach: ONE to LOTS*

Here you'll be offering some sort of an online membership where they pay per month for a content library. It could be a membership in a course or just live teaching. It could be dripped content (meaning you only give one video per day/week/month, etc.) Or all the content could be available for them to binge watch and consume.

The difference in group coaching is primarily that it's not live; it's all prerecorded content, though that is not a rule. Some coaches with membership groups go live and teach content to their entire group. The time period is usually month-to-month, though you could offer a lifetime membership or yearly discount to increase revenues.

## Group Coaching
*Income: $$ (Low to Moderate) | Reach: ONE to a FEW*

With group coaching you will be offering a similar model to the membership—it's you teaching a group, but it's often only a few (4-50 clients) rather than a large membership, some of which number in the thousands. It can be for a general theme or a challenge—meaning it's a very specific outcome and time (like six weeks to better mental health, or lose six pounds in six weeks).

You have an opportunity to have a more intimate relationship with the clients and can often do hot-seat teaching, where you bring up one (or every) client and use them as a teaching example for the rest of the group. The time frame is usually from six weeks to six months. For specific outcomes, the shorter the better (ideally less than six weeks).

## YOUR OFFER

## Accountability Coaching

*Income: $$-$$$ (moderately to mid-range) | Reach: ONE to a FEW*

Accountability coaching is about bringing procrastination to awareness, as well as providing support, guidance, tips, and mainly social pressure on tasks your clients want to accomplish. You can do this through one-on-one coaching or coaching a small intimate group. It can involve some traditional coaching, but often the biggest value clients get out of it is the pressure knowing that you will be asking them, "Did you do XYZ" as you promised?"

Depending on the client, this can be incredibly valuable, so the price will depend on your Dream Client Identity and how severely inaction is impacting their lives. Time frames are usually from six weeks to six months.

## Traditional/Mindset Coaching

*Income: $$-$$$ (moderate to mid range)| Reach: One-to- One*

Traditional or mindset coaching is what many people think of as coaching. It's a one-on-one session where the client and coach meet on a weekly or bi-monthly basis. There may be an outcome in mind, but the focus is more about the process of the coaching—creating a consistent safe space where the client can learn about themselves and acquire the tools needed to achieve their goals.

Though some coaches offer a per-session fee, I recommend packages of a minimum of three-to-six months as this gives you more reliable income and time to affect change with your client.

## COACHING LEADS FORMULA

# High Performance Coaching
*Income: $$$$+ (high) | Reach: One-to-One*

When I say high performance, I mean a specific, advanced hybrid of mentorship and coaching. The coach has gotten the result that the client wants—better health, mindset, leadership, sales skills, etc. I know some coaches will argue with me and say they're all different, and they are. But in one respect they're all very similar: the coach has a very specific, best-in-class ability to help the client achieve extraordinary results and charges accordingly.

High performance coaching is often an intense style of coaching that is primarily one-on-one, though I've seen coaches do this with small teams as well. The income potential is very high, but so is the skill, process, and systems needed—the clients want BIG results. It's often a contracted period of several months to a year.

# Breakthrough Coaching
*Income: $$$$+ (high) | Reach: One-to-One*

Aside from some select group coaching (a.k.a. challenges), breakthrough coaching is different from many other types as it's specifically outcome-oriented for the client. Once the outcome is achieved, the coaching is mostly over. Whatever the client says is the specific goal is how you will know when the breakthrough has been achieved. It requires a great deal of flexibility with the coaching techniques because you will often be facing a lifetime of habits and patterns that will need to be unwound before the client can move forward and achieve the desired outcome.

The advantage to a coach is the time involved—there isn't a lot of ongoing coaching. You work with the clients in short, intense bursts; teach them the tools; and empower them to create new, powerful habits and patterns. However, it can be bursts of long hours for the coach and the client. But when you've been depressed and self-abusive for years, what's a few days of work worth to feel like you're worthy of love again?

# Pricing

Do you think you're charging too much? Or do you think you're not charging enough? The most common answer I hear from coaches is, "I'm not charging what I'm worth **but I'm afraid to charge more**."

There's that problem called fear again! What a wonderful teacher fear must be to visit us so frequently. You might not think fear is the problem. You might tell yourself the problem is "The market won't support higher prices," or "I don't have the experience to support fees like that," or even the good old "If I raise my prices my clients will leave." Let's be totally honest though—all of those boil down to fear of some kind.

If this applies to you, I invite you to dig into that fear to find its root. Is it the fees, the money, the approval...what? That is for you to discover, and I encourage you to dig deeply because you'll find a wonderful freedom once that fear is rooted out for good!

For now though, I only want to talk about money as an exchange medium of value. It's not a dollar, pound, or euro, it's value being exchanged. Although I know you're going to have a comfort thermostat to measure the actual amount to charge, consider some things you might not have thought of before when determining your prices.

I remember that my fifth grade teacher said, "You will get out of this class how much you put into it." Well I believe that coaching is the same. However much your client is willing to put into the process of discovery and the work of the process is how much value they will receive (with your guidance, of course). The drive to make that change has to come from your client. You, as their coach, cannot give that to them.

## COACHING LEADS FORMULA

If your client puts in the work without having to be cajoled or coerced, that's fantastic but I think that's a rare client. Even though there are always exceptions, most clients need some external motivation to get started, keep going, or even finish. Why do I say that? Because there's a world of information out there available to everyone. If your clients truly wanted to change, they could go find the information from somewhere, somehow, or from someone else they found online and their problem would be solved.

Their problem is not a lack of resources. It's a lack of motivation.

I'm betting they found you and saw in you a shortcut or a way to solve their problem FASTER. However, as you know, that road is full of bumps, twists, and turns that are often hidden from view and are very rarely comfortable. Few people are willing to go down Discomfort Drive unless they feel it's absolutely necessary. Until they reach that point, they will continue living in their discomfort just as they have all their lives up to that point.

You must make change necessary for them. This is how you can help them. To take it from desirable to necessary you need some sort of leverage, and money is a massively motivating force for most people.

When your client willingly pays a higher price, they will value your coaching that much more. It's human nature. "You get what you pay for." That axiom is ingrained in our society. To undercharge risks being undervalued and taken for granted. Worst of all, it deprives your client of the transformation they deserve and want.

If you don't want to charge much and your dream client can't pay more than the minimum, I'm all for it, but realize there will be a cost to you. In order to survive, you will have to serve more and more clients. In the end you will have a very full schedule with not much time for anything else. You'll probably be burned out and have no creativity to grow your business because you're exhausted.

## YOUR OFFER

### But how *much*?

Do you remember the old fairytale of Goldilocks? How she thought one porridge was too cold, another too hot, and then one JUST right? That's a good formula to follow when considering pricing. Especially if you're displaying it publicly. Your prospects won't want to think they're cheap, but they might not be willing (or convinced yet of your value) to commit to the top tier. You want a price that's affordable but also a stretch for them. They need to be a little uncomfortable so they stay committed to the process and you.

If your client is price shopping, they're not looking for actual value (yet). Change hasn't become a necessity for them (yet). Let's say you charge half of what another coach does and you're equally (if not more) qualified. But you want to reach a demographic that needs your help. In order for you to make the same as the other coach, you will have to work twice as much. That will cut out any time for friends, family, or working ON the business so it can grow and expand. The other coach (the one who is less qualified) will have lots of time and money to improve their education as well as time to reflect and improve and innovate. Pretty soon, they will leave you in the dust and be much happier in the process!

Why wouldn't you want what that other coach now has? Why should you not have more free time—and more importantly, the freedom to choose?

Perhaps you want to charge more but don't know how to justify that price. It's a good idea to know what the market is charging but only for information. Those other coaches aren't you. What you bring is unique and you can't really compare because your services are different by the simple fact that YOU are different.

## COACHING LEADS FORMULA

So how do you put a price on your value? If you add up all the time and money you've spent to arrive at your current level of experience (in life and professionally), I'll bet you'd be shocked.

Between school, certification, and personal struggles, it all adds up to a pretty big number. Let's say you were an economics major in school but you're now coaching. You shouldn't count the cost of getting that econ degree, right? Wrong—because it informs your decisions and values. It has made you who you are today. It is part of what makes you uniquely suited to help them.

How much does all that experience and education add up to? I'm sure it's a lot of money! Let's say it adds up to about $250,000, which may seem high, but remember, it's not just the cost of the education, it's also the full cost of your time. Now, you want to work twenty hours a week and still have a vacation each year, so that comes to roughly one thousand hours of working time each year. But you have to work ON the business, not only IN the business, so that thousand hours is actually about five hundred coaching hours per year. When you divide $250k by 500 hours, you come up with $500 an hour! See how easy that is?

Once you have created an undeniable certainty in your prospect's mind that the value you can and will deliver will help them overcome their challenges, they will agree to any price. On the other hand, if they remain unconvinced, you could name any price (including free) and they might still question it because you haven't sold them on the value.

Some coaches I've worked with are AMAZING coaches who just LOVE to help people, but it's often at the cost of their own survival. As noble as it may seem to lower your prices until everyone can afford them, there will always be people who are unable to afford your services. You will be tempted to cut them a special price. Then one will turn into two, which will turn into twenty because it gets easier with each one.

I love you for that! But I have a suggestion if that's a desire for you.

# YOUR OFFER

IF you're absolutely convinced someone needs and deserves (and will benefit) from your coaching, then create a nonprofit or a scholarship program. With that mechanism, you can have a certain number of slots available for help. Don't get sucked into doing it for everyone. Your services are valuable! You also need to ask them to be committed to the process by putting some skin in the game. That can be money, volunteering somewhere, donating, or whatever you think is appropriate so they're making the value equation balanced.

I know you want to serve. It's why you're a coach! You want to help others and make an impact in the world. That's why I love working with folks just like you. I know you want to help as many people as you can! Some of you may be tempted to lower your prices so everyone can benefit from your coaching, but remember: You can always lower your prices or offer more value as a bonus, but once you've quoted your prices to a lead, it's difficult to raise those prices.

There is one exception to that. If you are offering a time-sensitive special or if the time has passed, it's natural to raise your prices if your clients or prospects are getting more or they didn't take action on a discount.

If you start down the rabbit hole of "That's a lot per hour, etc.,"remember that your clients aren't paying for your TIME—they're paying for the TRANSFORMATION. So if you get caught up in the hourly wage trap, simply refocus on the transformation and forget about the cost.

COACHING LEADS FORMULA

# 16. Sales Psychology

We're on to the dreaded topic—SALES!

I know there are hundreds, if not thousands, of books written on sales. This book is not intended to be the only source of information on the topic. Sales is necessary. Learn it, practice it, embrace it!

Whether you know it or not, you're selling every day. It could be selling your husband or wife on who will pick up the kids from school. It could be selling the person ahead of you to let you cut in line because you're late and need to get a quick lunch. Or it could be a sales call with a client. We're selling every day—the only difference is what is being exchanged.

If you're like many coaches I've worked with (or most of the population), you probably don't like sales.

You probably like salespeople even less!

I have good news though: The Client Leads Formula makes sales EASY.

If you follow everything I've talked about and implemented even half of it, your sales conversations will be pretty easy.

## COACHING LEADS FORMULA

I can hear your disbelief, but it's true. Most people don't like salespeople because they get sold when they're not always ready to buy.

Think of it this way. Imagine you were at Six Flags and were standing in the waterpark, dripping wet, and having the best time because you just went down the water slide. I suddenly come up to you and offer to sell you a bottle of water. How much would you pay for it? Or would you even be interested in it with all that water surrounding you?

Now I want you to imagine you had taken a trip to Egypt to see the pyramids. You took a horse out to see these majestic monuments so you could get there faster. But a bee stung the horse and made it go crazy, carrying you farther and farther into the desert. Eventually after a few hours, the horse stopped, exhausted and tired. I suddenly come up to you and offer you a bottle of water. How much would you pay for it then? You didn't have any water with you because you thought you'd only be gone thirty minutes.

Did you see how you demonstrated instant value? Most people will sell on price alone, but everyone buys based on how valuable something is to them. If you demonstrate enough value, price doesn't matter.

By using the marketing assets you've created and effective timing, you will have a slam-dunk sale because you've demonstrated extreme value. If they're ready, it won't be a sales conversation—it will simply be the natural progression of how to help them.

Having said that, you still need to have a certain mindset—that you CAN help them and that you have the solution. Sometimes people will ask questions about the process, how you work, what tools you use, etc. I'd suggest asking them this: "If you were going to have surgery, would you inquire as to the suture size or the type of scalpel the surgeon will be using?" Of course not. Have the confidence that they will achieve their outcome, and they will trust you even more.

SALES PSYCHOLOGY

There is a progression to a sales conversation. One step leads to another and does so deliberately and methodically. If you follow the steps, your prospects will be ready for your coaching and it will be one of the easiest conversations you'll ever have.

Although there are entire books devoted to the sales process, I will outline how I approach a sales conversation below.

## Building Rapport

The first step is building rapport. The good news is that you've already done that prior to getting on the call with them. You've delivered value, told stories, given a lead magnet, been vulnerable—a lot of elements go into that process.

But now you've got to build rapport on the one-on-one conversation you're having with them. You can do that. You know how. Just be yourself, identify with their situation, share a little about your journey, and how you've been able to move past the struggle they're currently experiencing.

## Identifying Needs

The next step is identifying needs. You need to figure out, in their language, what they need. What is it they want? How is their life suffering as a result of their challenge? Find out how they're impacting others in their life. What is that challenge doing to their relationships, their goals, their dreams? Find out how it's holding them back.

Remember: The key here is to be curious. Ask lots of open-ended questions. Instead of asking, "Did that make you feel bad?" ask, "So tell me about what happened after. How did that make you feel?" It asks for stuff (the "what") and feelings too.

## Pro Tip: Closed Eye

Not all clients will be able to access their feelings. You can help them by asking them to do a closed-eye process—essentially a guided meditation.

Walk them through the process of identifying what life looks like if they continue without changing. How bad is life in one, five, ten years.

Encourage them to tell you what they're seeing and experiencing.

Then have them imagine life with what they want—they've achieved their goal and life is good—in fact it's GREAT! Get them to share what they're seeing/experiencing there too. Take notes of these things so you can refer to them later in the process.

This accomplishes a few things. One, it gets them following your direction. Two, it previews what coaching will be like with you. Three, it gets them accessing their emotions, which is how people make decisions. Four, it gets agreement, and the more small yeses we get, the easier a commitment will be.

---

Remember how most people make a decision to buy on emotions but then justify it by using facts? Some people will jump right into the facts as a way of avoiding making a decision. It's up to you here and now to get them committed emotionally. You're not at the facts stage yet. Focus on the emotional impact of the challenges and their eventual consequences. It's better to get a "Heck no!" than a "Maybe," and getting the emotional buy-in helps avoid "Maybe."

If you need to, ask how inaction has impacted them today and what it will look like in the future. Ask how good or bad their life will be if they don't do anything other than what they've been doing.

SALES PSYCHOLOGY

# Link the Need to Coaching

Once you know their pain points and their big challenges, you need to link it to your coaching. How will signing up with you today solve their challenge and make their life better? Since they shared what their dreams and great life would look like, you could probably easily link your coaching to that outcome. When you link their needs to your solution, it's pretty easy to ask for the sale.

The final step will be to ask for the sale, or better yet, assume the sale by asking them how they'd like to pay—check or card.

# Objections

If you've gotten this far in the conversation, they're probably close to making a commitment and putting their money down. A few will just sign up right there, but others will need a little more guidance.

Some will have questions still and that's natural. The first step is to agree with them. Don't turn it into an adversarial situation.

Agree by saying something like, "Wow, that makes sense. I understand where you're coming from," or "I know how you feel," or "I realize it's an investment (notice I didn't say 'it's expensive' - I framed it as an investment in their future/happiness/success)."

Then immediately ask them if they want to end the conversation. It puts you back in the driver's seat. Questions control the flow. The person who is asking the questions will ultimately be able to determine where the conversation is going. Asking them if they'd like to end the conversation does a few things:

- It gives them a choice and makes them feel like they're in control (allows them to open up more)

- It gets them to agree (we want micro commitments)

- It lets you know they DO want to commit

- It assures them you're not going to push them

# COACHING LEADS FORMULA

Use your own words, but say something like, "I'm not a salesperson and I don't want you to commit if you're not ready. Would you like to end the call/conversation now, or would you like to talk a little more?"

More than likely they'll want to continue talking. They've invested and committed this far—remember Newton's First Law: Those that are in motion tend to stay in motion!

When they present their objection, it's useful to act confused. Ask them to clarify what they mean. "What do you mean by _____?" This lets you unpack what the real objection is.

Many buyers will have some form of objection, and I find that most objections fall into four camps:

Money: Of course, they need to truly be financially able to afford it, but you can present the value of not taking your coaching. The physical, financial, emotional, relationship cost of continuing doing what they're doing. How will that impact their lives and happiness?

- **Trust:** This simply means you haven't built enough rapport and demonstrated your value yet. That can easily be remedied by backing up in the conversation and asking them where they feel they lost confidence in what you're demonstrating for them.

- **Need:** Usually this has more to do with their perception. "I don't know how it can benefit me," meaning they're not convinced it can work for them specifically. It could work for others, but not them. They may simply need more qualifications, but they may also get some sort of benefit (secondary gain) by having the problem. An example might be if perhaps the person is overweight, they get lots of attention related to their weight, and are worried that if they lose the weight, they'll lose the attention. If this is the case, you can either get more leverage with the consequences of inaction or determine that they may not yet be ready to change.

## SALES PSYCHOLOGY

- **Urgency:** Similar to need, this might simply mean that the prospect is not a client at this time. Giving them time, getting to know them, and continuing to stay in touch is the way to continue to build the relationship so that when it is time, you're there to help them.

Most objections are rooted in money and value.

With money, in addition to what I suggested above, you can ask, "Is it the lump sum that's a problem? If we spread it out over several payments would that help you budget better?" If money is an objection, you can remove it to get to the root of the issue by offering something like PayPal financing, which lets you pay for something over six months with 0% interest.

If someone has the confidence (or habit) of asking for a lower price, you can reframe it by asking them, "If I lowered the investment right now, would you trust me less or more to deliver for you." That will usually shut down any negotiation on price.

When you encounter a value objection, just go back to the beginning of the conversation, and ask them about their goals. You can be a little confused here: "I'm confused here. Do you mind if I ask you a few questions so I can get clear?" (You're getting another micro commitment.) "You just said you wanted to _____. What's changed in the last two or three minutes?"

With any objection, your job is to be flexible in your responses. Constantly ask yourself, "What if _____ wasn't a problem?" and ask them a question to reframe it so the problem is able to be overcome.

Using metaphors in objection-handling can be very useful. You can address the objection without putting the person on the defense. "That reminds me of a client I had— "

137

## COACHING LEADS FORMULA

No matter the objection, you're the one who is writing the prescription. If you come from authority, curiosity, compassion, and confidence, you'll be able to sign them up for your coaching!

Worst case: If they decide not to sign up during this conversation, ask them if you can follow up with them in the future and see how they're doing. *Then do it! Put it on your calendar!* File your notes from this conversation so you can review them before that follow-up call.

Some clients take several conversations to get to the point where they are ready. It's not always about your selling skills, your coaching, or even the price. It could just be that they're not yet ready to change. By doing your follow up, you'll eventually be their choice!

One final note - when you run into objections and see a pattern, write them down and find a good response to them that allows the client to move forward. Write them on slips of paper, or somewhere you can see them during the call. This way you don't get stumped by any of the common objections - you know already how to respond to them!

BACK OFFICE

# 17. Back Office

Even though you love coaching, it's not all you have to do. In order to run a successful business, there are lots of tasks that fall outside of the strict coaching hours. Mostly they fall into two categories: getting clients and keeping them.

Getting clients is related to marketing and sales calls—that's what we've been talking about up until now. However, keeping clients is related to tracking client progress and how to hold on to clients—that's what we're going to explore now.

## Onboarding Process

Once you've accepted someone's trust, you have a solemn duty to protect and nurture that trust. In essence, you are reborn in your client's eyes. The relationship is completely different now. Because they've given you something of value, the expectations have changed. You have an opportunity to make a great impression with your new client.

That trust might have been born from giving you an email address or money so that they are now a client. From your first official communication though, you've begun to establish a new type of relationship focused on how you're going to help them with their transformation. Before, they were curious or interested, but now that they're serious and committed, you need to respect that shift and change the tone of your conversation.

## COACHING LEADS FORMULA

The process of onboarding a client is your opportunity to deepen the relationship you've already built. Now you get to expose them to the inner workings, to see some of the magic behind the curtain.

Now is also a great time to discover the potential non-clients who wouldn't be a great fit. Remember, this is for someone who has raised their hand and said, "I'm interested in your services or products." They may have already pulled the trigger and put money down, but more than likely this is someone who is going to apply for that free coaching session. Some of those will be just tire-kickers, but here's your chance to see who is truly committed and who is just browsing.

Think of the marketing process as a conversation with an ever-increasing level of commitment, eventually culminating in a purchase or sale. Some of the milestones along the way are small—like silently agreeing with a video, commenting on a post, or perhaps downloading a lead magnet in exchange for their email.

Once a prospect starts to fill out your application form, that is a big milestone because they are willing to commit with their time, vulnerability, and sometimes money. In essence, they're saying, "I trust you fully." The application is a series of questions, and I LOVE how the right questions can really direct where and what someone is focusing on. The application is designed with a series of questions to get them focusing on the right things so you can best help them.

The application form is so you can learn what their challenges are, what kind of client they will be, and get them to further commit to the process of working with you. It's designed to get you the information you need.

One of the most important aspects of the application is to qualify them so you can really know if they're a client at this time (not everyone is ready to be a client yet even though they are at the application stage). You want to know what they've tried in the past and what/how will you do/be different?

# BACK OFFICE

You also want to show some of your personality too! Be silly and let your unique style show through. Personally, I like to ask what they think their superpower is because it gives them an opportunity to really use their imagination and I can discover one of their desires, even if it's a fantasy.

Things to ask in your application:

1. Basics like name, pronoun (if applicable), age, profession, address, social media (if you want to include shout-outs)

2. Biggest challenge and how it's impacting their life

3. Biggest goal/dream and what getting it will do for them

4. What they have tried in the past that worked

5. What they have tried in the past that didn't work

6. How they will know they've received value

7. What their expectations of you are if they get behind on their commitments to you

8. Include fun questions, a.k.a. favorite dessert, superhero, song, artist—let your personality show through here

    1. Qualify them with some question like: Are you willing to invest at least $1,000 in your personal development to get rid of your problem/challenge and achieve your goal?

    2. Do you understand I can't do this process for you, that you must be willing to put in the work and endure discomfort as part of the process?

After you've accepted a new client, you want to make sure to continue that amazing experience they've begun with you. Your welcome packet is the way you can do that. In it, you want to do two things: pre-frame what is going to happen next in your process and remember to make it fun too!

# COACHING LEADS FORMULA

A welcome packet might include:

- **Pre-frame next steps** - Outline what the next few steps will be doing for them and give them any further information you might need to convey.

- **Communication expectations** - Make sure to let them know how and how often to communicate with you. If you reply only via email, let them know. Or if you have a limit on one-on-one questions, state that. Also let them know when you will reply to them and what they can expect.

- **Have fun and be unexpected** - For many of you who will be charging more than $2,000, my feeling is that with a price point of that amount, you might want to send a physical gift to welcome them. That could be anything—a hat, a journal, a T-shirt, or even personalized wall art with their values! I'm not suggesting spending a lot, but 1-2% of what they've paid is reasonable. Trust me, if they see it constantly and it reminds you of them, it'll pay for itself many times over.

- **FAQ** - What are the common questions you get?

- **Quick Start Guide** - Perhaps include a beginner's video course explaining the first steps in your process.

- **Common misconceptions** - Things to start doing ASAP.

- **Cancellation and/or refund policy** - No matter how good our communication and planning are, things will come up. You need to have clear boundaries about what happens when your client either has to reschedule or misses an appointment. How many times will you reschedule or allow them to have a freebie when they miss?

BACK OFFICE

- **Liability waiver** - Depending on what type of coaching you're doing, you may need to have this in order to go over the potential risks so they release any liability you may have if anything happens as a result of your coaching.
  You want to have this reviewed by an attorney, but also purchase liability insurance because a waiver won't be enough to protect you or pay your attorney's fees if anything truly serious does happen.

- **Privacy policy** - Some clients don't care but others are extremely private and may ask for a nondisclosure agreement. It will depend on the client and their level of trust and comfort.

- **Contract** - It is my belief that we live up to what is expected of us. When we expect more from ourselves or know others expect more from us, we rise to meet that expectation. Occasionally you will have a client who refuses to do the work, and having a contract can create consequences of that refusal. I suggest a basic contract that asks the client to work as hard as they possibly can and to communicate if anything is unclear. That way you can always refer to the agreement if they don't show up the way you know they need to. Additionally, if you're doing any kind of mindset coaching, this is a clear opportunity for them to acknowledge that this is NOT therapy and have them signify they understand that in writing.

# Tracking Client Progress

Because this book is meant to cover life coaching as well as health and wellness coaching, there are many things to consider within your specific field and niche, which could be a book unto itself. However, I feel that tracking client progress is essential to ANY coaching business. No matter your field or niche, it's important because you need to know what is working and what is not.

# COACHING LEADS FORMULA

Tracking also gives you an easy tool to use at the time of renewal to point back and say, "Wow, look at all you accomplished!" and easily demonstrate your value. It also gives you an opportunity to mention the goals or milestones that haven't yet been hit or accomplished.

Many clients will go through their weeks and not really notice the cumulative changes that are happening in their lives. This is your opportunity to highlight them.

If their goal is to make one million dollars and they've only made $97,000, that's still a huge win, especially if they'd never made more than $50,000 before. Perhaps they took a vacation they'd been dreaming of for ten years, which is a massive milestone to celebrate. Remind them of that vacation!

Or if they have a goal of losing 100 lb, but they've *only*" lost 57 lbs - that's a HUGE win for them. It also gives you an opportunity to track other things, like maybe they've had to get a whole new wardrobe because their clothes no longer fit them! That's huge!

Tracking client progress is important. It gives them something to look at when their focus goes to frustration or anxiety. It allows them to reinforce what is working and see that your coaching is working.

## Retaining Clients

Even though the title of this book is about getting leads (a.k.a. new prospects to become clients), it's far easier and infinitely cheaper to keep an existing client than to go out and find a new one. Or even to renew an old client who you haven't worked with in some time.

Cold leads take money and time to acquire. With existing (and past) clients, you've already done much of the work. They know, like, and trust you already—plus they know you get results!

The more clients you are able to keep, the more consistent your income will be. Depending on how you work, that could be signing up for another package, implementing a new routine because of new goals, or creating another breakthrough in another area of life.

## BACK OFFICE

I understand part of your process is (I hope) giving your clients new tools and mindsets to implement to make their lives better. Even though it may seem counterintuitive to keep a client if you've helped them solve their challenges, here's the beautiful thing: There's always a new level to achieve. And ironically, because *you're* growing, you're always going to have something new to teach and help them with!

So, how do you keep them onboard and working with you?

I'm glad you asked!

The best way to retain a client is to help them achieve great results! Help them reach the goals they want and continue to deliver value. You want them to feel amazing by working with you. In the process, you can also tease and occasionally mention the next level and remind them about how people live up to what is expected of them. You want to show you care in the words you use, the consistency of communication, and occasionally in unexpectedly fun ways.

Celebrate with them when they get a win! Give them permission to look back and notice the accomplishment. If you're anything like me and the coaches I've worked with, you'll probably notice clients celebrate for a short while the BIG win and forget about the hard journey to get there. Help them recognize the transformation they've achieved in their life!

As I mentioned earlier, one way to celebrate is with an unexpected gift that is relevant and personal to them and the accomplishment. Help them commemorate the accomplishment. There's a very good psychological reason organizations give awards, certificates, medals, etc. It demonstrates a specific accomplishment and a reason to celebrate the new person they are after achieving that goal.

## COACHING LEADS FORMULA

Another way to celebrate them is through a social media shout-out. Personal trainers use this to great degree. It's a public acknowledgment of their achievement, but it also demonstrates to others YOUR expertise and grace in pointing to and (genuinely) celebrating their achievement. One caveat here though, is to be sure you have their explicit (written or otherwise recorded) permission to share something publicly.

What milestones can you set up in your group coaching or one-on-one coaching that will allow you to create a reason to celebrate with your clients?

**Gift Tips:**

- Make it relevant - Have it be related to your coaching as well as the client's accomplishment.

- Personalized - You want it special and made specifically for them. You can engrave something, stitch it, or have it painted. There's suggestions on how to do this in the resources section.

- Usage - You want whatever it is to be frequently used or seen. Things like a coffee mug or custom wall art that they see every day (ask them to take a picture of it hanging up and share the picture with you!).

- Quality - You want something that's affordable but nice enough that they will want to show it off. I personally like to spend between $25 and $50 on a custom gift (shipping excluded).

A note on billing systems: You want to put your billing on auto-renew rather than one-time payments. That way you won't have to have an awkward conversation with your client about the upcoming renewal—it'll already be locked in (with an opt-out option, of course). Whichever software you are using—Stripe, Paypal or something else—I'm sure it's there.

BACK OFFICE

# Virtual Offices

With everything that's happened in the world due to the pandemic, it's understandable to have clients meet you virtually. This creates a huge opportunity and also a huge cost savings!

Before, you had to find a space to meet clients in person. It could have been a conference room, a rented office space, a private room at a gym, or a dedicated space at your home. All of those options could get pretty expensive. Not to mention the added time in the process that you had to spend commuting to and from the work space.

But now, you are able to meet them on Zoom, through Facetime, even an old fashioned telephone call can work - you get to decide what works best. And all at a fraction of the cost!

If you want to work remotely, there's never been a better time in human history to be able to do so! Perhaps you enjoy hiking in the remote mountains. Well, go hiking in the morning and see clients in the afternoon. Or maybe you like to dance the tango in Argentina. Dance the night away and see clients after your afternoon nap. Perhaps location doesn't matter but you'd like to get as many clients as possible. Then find clients across the globe and be able to connect with them from 5:00 a.m. until 10:00 p.m. (if you choose).

The world is your oyster now—you aren't tied down to time zones or continents anymore. Today, you can see clients from all over the world anytime of the day from practically any location in the world.

Maybe traveling is your thing. One day you can have a client call from New York, and then travel to London for a call the next day. The day after that you could be helping a client from your hotel room in Rome, Italy!

As I've been working to finish up this book, I've been working on the book AND still taking client calls - all while traveling all across Europe on a much needed vacation after the pandemic-induced travel bans.

## COACHING LEADS FORMULA

Don't let borders, time zones or physical space stop you from being able to work. As long as you have an internet or phone connection, you are able to work with clients! In fact, during my travels, I learned many countries are offering what is known as a "Digital Nomad" visa. Meaning if you earn your money outside of the country of residence, you can stay for a long time - in Spain you can stay for up to five years!

I also encourage you to outsource yourself - not everything will require *your* time and attention. Is it something that is a one-time problem? Is it unique? Then by all means shoot an email and make a decision how you want to respond. But if it's a question or issue you see repeated, I encourage you to hire a virtual assistant to field those issues. You probably already respond to them in a pretty routine method anyway. Why not hire an assistant so you can focus on either building the business or doing what you love?

Being able to work from home, from an office, or from the airport is a unique blessing. As a coach you have that ability. If travel is a passion of yours as it is for me, I highly encourage you to see how you might be able to incorporate that (if you're not already doing that) into your business today. Not only will it save you time and money, but it will also give you the freedom that few in the world have today!

For additional help on what we've been discussing, I've created a list of resources that can help you. You'll find recommended books, tools, programs and additional training. To learn more, go to: https://getcfl.com/book

# 18. Testimonials

In today's world, it is essential to provide social proof. Without it, many people become wary of working with you. It could easily be the deciding factor whether a client chooses you over another coach.

But asking for testimonials can be uncomfortable, especially if you have to follow up in order to get the testimonial. So how do you get it and when is the best time to ask for it?

This book is all about creating systems that allow you to drive more revenue and clients without you having to do repetitive work. There are many systematic ways of doing this for reviews as well—often with Google and Facebook. You probably get an email a week asking you to write a review or leave feedback after you've bought something online. You can implement the same type of system into your business. Set up an automated email that gets sent out every three months or so. If Amazon is using it, you know it works! Tell your client to expect a survey of some sort to help you improve your services.

One exception here is if a client gets a huge win. When that happens, ask for feedback right then. There's no better time to get a testimonial than right at the moment when they are excited and celebrating!

## COACHING LEADS FORMULA

The simplest way to generate a review is to have clients fill out your Google or Facebook reviews. But to get a higher quality review, you can ask them to fill out an online survey. They're super simple to set up and there are lots to choose from. It's important to keep the survey short. The best surveys are only two or three questions. Remember that time is valuable, and you can always include an invitation to give more feedback via a phone call if you want.

Here's what to ask in your survey:

1. What's two or three things you love about the coaching?

2. What's one thing that could be different?

3. What is one thing that would make this EVEN better that I haven't done yet?

Easy, super short and to the point. When you send it, make sure to mention that it won't take more than five minutes to fill out and that it only has two or three questions that will give you guidance on how to better serve THEM in the future and grow as a coach as well.

If you have asked them to do a video testimonial and they are willing to do it, then it's really only those three things they need to talk about. I know people get nervous about doing a video testimonial but they are incredibly powerful, so I suggest at least asking for it.

Another benefit of a video testimonial is that it can serve dual purposes—you can use the video or transcribe the text from it and use it on printed materials also. Ask the client for a headshot and permission to use the photo. It creates additional authority if someone is willing to let you use their photo in relation to their words.

Similar to the storytelling framework I mentioned earlier, I ask my clients to think about three things for the video:

1. **Before:** What was the pain/frustration/challenge you were experiencing before we worked together? How did it impact your life?

## TESTIMONIALS

2.  **During:** What was the coaching like, how is my coaching different from others you've worked with (if applicable), and when did you realize the coaching was working?

3.  **After:** What does your life look like now—what goals or dreams have you been able to do or have? What does it feel like to be rid of that pain/frustration/challenge?

It doesn't have to be complex or long (could be as little as 60 seconds), just remind them: before, during, after. They can always redo it, as many times as they need, if they feel nervous. Today's phones have great cameras and are perfect for doing a testimonial.

This is the essence of user-generated content —meaning it's content you can use that is not created by you, but rather by your clients. It's the ultimate social proof!

One final note: Make life easy on yourself and include a checkbox that links to your terms and conditions which allows you to use their content. You can find examples of the UGC permissions agreements from your attorney or online.

# COACHING LEADS FORMULA

WRAPPING IT UP

# 19. Wrapping it Up

In this book we've covered a lot of material. I'm proud of you for having stuck through all the way to the end!

So, what have we gone over?

- How coaching really is a business, how you need to think like a business owner, and how nothing can get in your way if you have that mindset.

- The key to your business and coaching success is having consistent revenue and how that revenue is generated by developing rapport with your prospects.

- The value of storytelling, and specifically how to craft YOUR story, your signature story. You also learned how to adapt it with different clients and use it to build instant rapport and credibility.

- Lead magnets and landing pages—how they can literally transform your business and have clients clamoring for your services. All without you having to lift a finger.

- How the various price points will allow you to easily reach $60,000 a year in consistent revenue, all while only working about 15 hours a week.

153

## COACHING LEADS FORMULA

- How your extra time can now be used to build your business well beyond $60k—or spend time doing things you value and love.

- The sales cycle, how to approach objections, and how easy the sales conversation will be once you've developed a months-long rapport with your leads.

- We even talked about how to develop the best testimonials and keep clients, so you don't have to go searching for more to fill your calendar!

I wrote this book because I truly want the world to be a better place to live for everyone. I believe it can start with you and the tools and skills you can teach your clients. You can't do that, though, if you are only doing it in your spare time, or worse, if you stop coaching because it doesn't provide the necessary income.

I hope you have found what we have covered helpful, but there's more—an important aspect I've really neglected to mention up until now: implementation.

How do you implement this? I know there was a lot of content and many exercises here. The last thing I'd want you to do is to get overwhelmed and have this book simply gather dust.

I want the information used so you can be out there changing lives!

I suggest you go back through and do the exercises again. Yes, you might have already done them, but doing them again won't hurt anything. "Repetition is the mother of learning," as Zig Ziglar said.

Because you now have a fresh perspective from which to do the exercises, go back and do them again, but with much deeper detail and commitment. Take the notes—there should be pages of them!

## WRAPPING IT UP

Give yourself a week to complete each major task. That way you can go back and forth with a designer or give yourself the space and time to do it yourself.

- **Week 1:** Dream Client Work
- **Week 2:** Conversation Hook and Hero's Journey
- **Week 3:** Landing Page and Thank You Page
- **Week 4:** Lead Magnet
- **Week 5:** Email Setup

If you give yourself a week for each major landmark, you should be able to get all this accomplished in less than six weeks (with a little wiggle room added in). How would you like to completely transform your coaching business in a little less than a month and a half?

I'd say that's a no brainer!

I'd also suggest holding yourself accountable by posting something out there or setting a goal publicly with friends. That way they can hold your feet (very gently) to the fire if you're not following through on what you said you would do.

I'd like for you to do the same as you'd have a sales prospect do—imagine yourself one year from today. You've done the work, set up one or maybe even two different lead magnets and email sequences. You might have a few ads running to those landing pages. Every week you have at least half a dozen well-qualified sales conversations. You didn't have to lift a finger to set up those sales calls—they simply came from your email list that is growing at a healthy rate with each week.

## COACHING LEADS FORMULA

What does your life look like? How do you feel being able to help those people who are ready and want your coaching? What are you able to do now that you have lots of free time? Who do you get to spend that time with? What adventures are you able to go on now that you can afford them from a financial and time sense?

As I wrote this book, I found it very helpful to imagine you, my friend, not only making a difference in the world but also being happier and more fulfilled. Each day as I sit to write, I picture you and that amazing life you're leading.

So, what are the first three things you're committed to doing to bring about that new version of reality for you, your clients, your friends, and your family?

RESOURCES

# 20. Resources

Because resources, tools, and technology are constantly evolving, I've decided to include ongoing and updated links to things I consider valuable on my website. For ideas on gifts, website hosts, social media tools, video content, financing options, or email providers, go to:

https://coachingleadsformula.com/book-resources

Made in the USA
Las Vegas, NV
04 October 2023

78564927R00100